The Manager as Politician

**Recent Titles in
The Manager as...**

The Manager
as Politician

Jerry W. Gilley

The Manager as...

Westport, Connecticut
London

Library of Congress Cataloging-in-Publication Data

Gilley, Jerry W.
   The manager as politician / Jerry W. Gilley.
        p.   cm. — (The manager as..., ISSN 1555-7480)
   Includes index.
   ISBN 0-275-98590-3
   1. Office politics. 2. Organizational behavior. 3. Executive ability.
4. Management. I. Title. II. Series.
   HF5386.5.G55   2006
   658.4'09—dc22   2005026162

British Library Cataloguing in Publication Data is available.

Library of Congress Catalog Card Number: 2005026162
ISBN: 0-275-98590-3
ISSN: 1555-7480

First published in 2006

Praeger Publishers, 88 Post Road West, Westport, CT 06881
An imprint of Greenwood Publishing Group, Inc.
www.praeger.com

Printed in the United States of America

The paper used in this book complies with the
Permanent Paper Standard issued by the National
Information Standards Organization (Z39.48–1984).

10 9 8 7 6 5 4 3 2 1

Contents

Publisher's Note

The backbone of every organization, large or small, is its managers. They guide and direct employees' actions, decisions, resources, and energies. They serve as friends and leaders, motivators and disciplinarians, problem solvers and counselors, partners and directors. Managers serve as liaisons between executives and employees, interpreting the organization's mission and realizing its goals. They are responsible for performance improvement, quality, productivity, strategy, *and* execution—through the people who work for and with them. All too often, though, managers are thrust into these roles and responsibilities without adequate guidance and support. MBA programs provide book learning but little practical experience in the art of managing projects and people; at the other end of the spectrum, exceptional talent in one's functional area does not necessarily prepare the individual for the daily rigors of supervision. This series is designed to address those gaps directly.

The Manager as... series provides a unique library of insights and information designed to help managers develop a portfolio of outstanding skills. From Mentor to Marketer, Politician to Problem Solver, Coach to Change Leader, each book provides an introduction to the principles, concepts, and issues that define the role; discusses the evolution of recent and current trends; and guides readers through the dynamic process of assessing their strengths and weaknesses and creating a personal development plan. Featuring diagnostic tools, exercises, checklists, case examples, practical tips, and recommended resources, the books in this series will help readers at any stage in their careers master the art and science of management.

ONE

Managers as Politicians: An Introduction

The negative images of politics and politicians often prevent people from actively engaging in political interactions and engagements (see chapter 6). Consequently, people tend to avoid them or dismiss them altogether, which may have a detrimental effect on their careers. Some people even believe that engaging in politics diminishes their effectiveness and/or gives the appearance of unethical or unseemly behavior. However, the ability to navigate politics well is an essential ingredient to the success of any manager. It is therefore critical that you develop a politically savvy approach to be an effective leader in your organization.

When politics gets heavy-handed, you should develop a radar system that will help you avoid serious political situations that diminish your credibility, influence, and effectiveness. Without such a system, you may find yourself in situations that can cost you your job. So it is imperative that you develop a sixth sense for such *political landmines*. Consider the following techniques commonly employed in organizational settings.

Sometimes organizational members play serious political games that indicate their true intentions. For example, a common technique is known as the *frozen-out strategy*. This occurs when people purposefully leave you out of a major project or job assignment even though you should be participating. This technique is commonly used by people who have difficulty with confrontation or lack the ability to be direct. Some people use this technique to assert their authority and power or as a means of putting you in your place.

Another example of heavy-handed politics is known as *poisoning the well*. This occurs when a person makes a concerted effort to alter another person's opinions of your competencies and abilities. It is effective because you cannot defend or refute the negative statements. Consequently, your reputation may be damaged forever unless someone informs you that such statements are being made.

Another technique, known as *damning by faint praise*, occurs when a person, rather than communicating exactly what he or she truly feels or believes, offers you a compliment expressed in such feeble terms that an unspoken negative opinion of your abilities is strongly implied. The person receiving the message is on his or her own to figure out the hidden agenda. Typically, the message is interpreted in the worst possible way, which ultimately diminishes your reputation, credibility, and/or influence. This result is exactly what the sender of the message desires and is why this technique is effective.

In most professional environments, *public put-downs* are not common, although they do occur. The public put-down is a publicly experienced insult, interruption, patronizing comment, blocking behavior, or criticism in which another party is challenging your competencies, thinking, and abilities. If this technique occurs, the political environment has evolved to a hostile state. Regardless, such actions can leave lasting scars and inflict emotional damage. Commonly, public put-downs occur because the aggressor lacks political or interpersonal skills or he or she is attempting to overtly destroy your credibility, reputation, and/or influence.

One of the most deceitful and manipulative techniques is known as *faking left, going right*. This technique occurs when a person intentionally conveys that a condition exists, but in reality, another condition is present. It is serious because it sets you up for failure. This technique can easily result in making you look foolish, with you having no way of explaining or defending your actions or decisions.

Most of these political landmines are covert and difficult to defend against. Therefore, your primary strategy for evading them is political awareness and observation. In this way, you are always looking for the conditions where landmines are present. Your best defense is to demonstrate that you are an alert political adversary, one ready for any contingency.

BECOMING A POLITICAL NAVIGATOR

Becoming a political navigator requires you to develop two types of competencies. They are (1) professional expertise, and (2) political skills.

To best illustrate this concept, visualize a bicycle. A bicycle has two wheels: a front and back wheel. The back wheel provides the power to propel the bicycle forward and represents your understanding of your business/organization, professional competency, and expertise. The back wheel symbolizes the skills, talents, abilities, expertise, and competencies for which the organization hired you in the first place. These competencies are used to enhance the organization's performance capacity and strategic position. On the other hand, the front wheel allows you the maneuver the bicycle through difficult situations and gives you the ability to avoid obstacles, potholes, and barriers in order to guide the bicycle to your final destination. The front wheel represents your political skills and competencies, which are critical when working with other people in your organization. These abilities are critical to building relationships, resolving conflicts, and negotiating positive outcomes. Quite simply, you need both front and back wheel competencies to become a successful political navigator.

Understanding the answers to four questions will determine whether you are capable of becoming a political navigator:

- What does it take to be politically effective?
- What are the roles and responsibilities of a political navigator?
- What are the competencies required to be politically effective?
- Are you aware of your political skills and abilities?

The answers to these questions determine what it means to be a professional. A "professional" is a person who is both competent (the first three questions) and fully aware of the *reasons* for that competence (the last question). When political interactions and engagements fail to accomplish their objective, a political navigator knows *why* they went wrong and what should be done to prevent failure in the future. A professional is what we call a *conscious competent* (Figure 1.1).

Many managers start at the bottom on the effectiveness quadrangle, as an *unconscious incompetent*. In fact, some managers do not have the competencies to perform as a political navigator (front or back wheel) and do not even know how to improve. Occasionally, through trial, error, and intuition, some managers master the knowledge and skills needed to be minimally effective and overcome incompetence.

Those who achieve success over time are *unconsciously competent*. That is, they do not know why they are good, and they do not know how to repeat the cycle or take corrective action if a political interaction or engagement gets off course. A *conscious incompetent* demonstrates performance that is inconsistent. While they know how to be politically astute, they elect to not put this knowledge into action. Unfortunately, many such managers never choose to improve and suffer the consequences of their inaction.

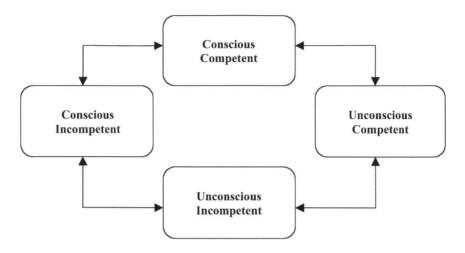

Figure 1.1. Becoming a Conscious Competent

As a political navigator, you are a conscious competent and you benefit your organization by

- creating a political environment based on understanding, acceptance, and involvement, which enhance rapport, trust and honesty, and self-esteeming behaviors;
- improving performance and efficiency;
- enhancing openness by encouraging cooperation and collaboration;
- fostering inclusiveness and engagement by developing a solution-oriented culture;
- cultivating communities of inquirers by allowing others the opportunity to participate openly during political interactions and engagements;
- enhancing creativity by encouraging innovative problem solving;
- enhancing communications and synergy by improving relationships, which results in a more collegial work environment.

Political navigators satisfy the needs of other people while positioning themselves in a more positive light within the organization. Accordingly, you enhance your credibility and the value of the services you provide within an organization and influence the direction of the organization. You develop relationships that are synergistic, mutually beneficial, and long-term oriented. These relationships require you to develop a responsive, value-added, client service orientation that better understands and anticipates other people's needs. Your primary benefit is increased influence within your firm.

Political navigators demonstrate the experience, capability, qualifications, competence, and people skills necessary to achieve results in a timely fashion, within budget, and according to quality specifications. Accordingly, you are an expert who understands the importance of interpersonal interaction, which can create conflict if not deal with appropriately. As such, you understand the human and organizational aspects of conflict and the numerous responses (fear, excitement, suspicion) and approaches available to successfully plan for, communicate, implement, monitor, and evaluate conflict resolution strategies (see chapters 3 and 4).

Becoming politically competent gives you the opportunity to develop personal relationships with employees, other managers, and organizational leaders. Alliances allow you to create trust and develop a shared vision of the future through a free exchange of information, ideas, and perceptions. Such partnerships promote establishment of working relationships based on aligned purpose, shared values, mutual support, and vision.

Political navigators demonstrate their willingness to intimately know those they serve, as well as enhance their ability to learn from others. Furthermore, partnerships are based upon the business and performance needs of other people, not merely shallow, meaningless, interpersonal exchanges (see chapters 3 and 4). Becoming a political navigator allows you to direct all your efforts at satisfying your clients (employees, senior managers and leaders, and other managers), including designing and developing political engagements in accordance with other people-expressed interests (see chapter 6).

Finally, becoming a political navigator produces economic utility, which is measured in terms of increased organizational performance, profitability, revenue, quality, or efficiency. Overall, political alliances afford you the opportunity to work in harmony for the purpose of improving the economic viability of the organization. A healthy organization benefits all.

UNDERSTANDING THE
POLITICAL INTERACTION PROCESS

A political navigator becomes the master of political interactions. In short, a political interaction is a conversation between you and another person designed to achieve a desired result while simultaneously meeting the interests and needs of all parties. It includes the sharing of information, interests, perspectives, needs, expectations, procedures, ideas, behavioral norms, methods of achieving a desired outcome, and rules of engagement. In short, political interactions are the tracks of political success. They carry you to your political destination while providing you the opportunity to enhance relationships, build credibility, and improve political effectiveness.

Let's examine the following political interaction: While attending a meeting regarding the implementation of a new compensation and benefits program within a large consulting firm, the human resource manager of the firm, Michael, is approached by the executive vice president (EVP) of business development, Melissa. In no uncertain terms, Melissa states that she is disappointed with client service in the firm and believes it is one of the reasons that the firm has been unable to increase its market share during the past few years. She further indicates that it is critical that the firm increase its revenues during the last quarter of the year because she is being pressured by the president and board of directors to do so. This will also demonstrate to the organizational leaders that the firm is moving in the right direction

Melissa asks Michael if he has any ideas that might be of assistance in her quest to improve revenues. She is convinced that all members of the organization should participate in a comprehensive customer service (CS) training program. She insists that this activity might very well be a means of creating a better CS philosophy within the firm.

Overwhelmed by the complexity of the conversation and its potential implications, Michael is reluctant to make any premature suggestions. He recommends that they meet later in the week to discuss the issue in further detail. This will give him the time to study the situation so that he can develop a better understanding of the circumstances. They continue to exchange pleasantries and, finally, agree on a time to meet later in the week.

Immediately after the meeting, Michael goes to his office and begins to examine internal documents that may provide him with a better understanding of the current situation facing the firm. After examining several documents, he decides that it might be wise to obtain another perspective on the situation. Next, he arranges a meeting with the chief financial officer (CFO) of the firm. During this confidential meeting, the CFO provides previously missing information that offers additional insight. Michael solicits advice and recommendations and then identifies an appropriate course of action.

Early the next morning, Michael is able to gather his thoughts and develop a comprehensive list of questions he will ask Melissa later in the week. He asks one of his respected colleagues to examine the list of questions and this person provides a few additional suggestions. Finally, Michael feels confident that he will be able to discuss Melissa's recommendation for comprehensive CS training in an informed, enlightened manner.

During the meeting with Melissa, Michael is able to participate in an informed dialogue that acknowledges her concerns but also challenges some of her assumptions. After addressing each of the questions Michael prepared for the meeting, they agree that the best way to proceed is to not immediately punish the employees with training, but to examine the situation more closely to determine whether or not a CS problem really exists. They decide to meet in a few weeks to discuss the parameters of the analysis, as well as to outline next steps.

This example illustrates how you can think politically (chapter 4) when asked to take actions that may or may not be appropriate. For many, a request for training from a senior member of the organization is reason enough to immediately take action. They would instantaneously assemble their staffs, set up project parameters, establish timelines, identify available resources, formulate a project schedule, and start the laborious task of identifying the most appropriate training program to deliver within the organization. But is this the correct decision? In most circumstances, it is not. Furthermore, such an action may not deliver the results needed and the EVP now has a convenient person to blame—a scapegoat, in other words—for the continued shrinkage in market share and the expenditures of valuable financial resources on a training program that fails to improve results. Finally, this is a classic example of a political interaction that, depending upon how it is handled, can either positively or negatively affect your credibility and influence in the organization

A political interaction is a *process* rather than a technique or outcome. Therefore, you direct your energies toward helping others understand the purpose of the political interaction and your roles and responsibilities during it. During such an interaction, you seek other people's opinions, suggestions, and recommendations regarding the best way of generating the desired outcome. As such, you do not advise or make decisions for others but seek agreement between them. This is accomplished by encouraging other people to appreciate their differences and complexities. Additionally, you improve participation by encouraging tolerance for ambiguity. Finally, you enhance confidence, expectation, and opportunity by encouraging others to discover their own solutions to problems. In short, you use a multitude of skills (relationship, communications, negotiation, observation, partnership, conflict resolution, and political thinking skills; see chapter 4) to encourage participation and provide guidance during political interactions to achieve a desire outcome.

Political navigators should not engage in political interactions unless they can clearly identify the motives that drive the exchange. By identifying the motives of individuals engaged in political interactions, future problems and difficulties can be avoided. To guard against simply reacting to the requests of clients, political thinking skills are essential (see chapter 4). If individuals' motives cannot be clearly identified, insights and advice should be solicited from other members of the organization. In this way, the integrity of the process and the political navigator's credibility remain protected.

Next, develop a working knowledge of the departments, divisions, and units within the organization. Since each group has its own mission, processes, and perspectives, as a political navigator, you discover their performance issues and major initiatives. As a result, you forge links with all the different parts of the organization.

Facilitating political interaction effectively is an art in that it offers you a unique opportunity to work along with and for people in a way that allows them to enhance and fulfill their responsibilities. It also allows you to be a *peaceful warrior* responsible for bringing about needed change through candid deliberations. Effective political interactions require you to eliminate unproductive or sabotaging behavioral patterns that will interfere with implementing needed change. It requires you to be vigilant and ready for action. It requires you protect other people from becoming casualties of a political engagement (see chapter 6) by being aware of the possible negative reaction others can have during such an event. Finally, effective political interactions mean guiding others through processes to achieve the desired outcomes. Some possible outcomes of a political interaction include the following:

- new learning
- performance improvement
- employee development
- conflict resolution
- creative problem solving and decision making
- strategic planning
- performance and change management processes

Purpose of Political Interactions

The primary purpose of political interactions is to assist others by helping them understand their concerns, expectations, thoughts, and fears. As such, as a political navigator, you help others maximize their learning about the organization and its people. Consequently, you become a facilitator to others by allowing them to explore and uncover their own knowledge, which is achieved by encouraging them to question, confront, and challenge their own assumptions about the situation at hand. This enables others to embrace and accept alternatives and differences.

Political interactions encourage problem solving through personal reflection and application. During a group political interaction, you help others to examine their behavior, which includes their ability to listen, provide feedback, generate solutions, plan alternatives, and challenge one another. Further, you relinquish some of your control. When you fail to do this, you reduce your effectiveness. Therefore, you relinquish such traditional managerial behaviors as controlling workflow, issuing detailed instructions, and micromanaging others to insure that they produce adequate outcomes. As a political navigator, you adopt new behaviors, such as facilitating and coaching others, which enhance people's self-esteem and confidence. During effective political interaction, you engage in several activities:

- helping others understand their needs, expectations, and interests
- employing coaching and facilitating skills
- encouraging responsibility for self-motivation and achieving organizational goals
- using participative and facilitative methods to resolve conflict
- inspiring a shared vision
- challenging processes by confronting, experimenting, and searching for opportunities

Improving Political Interactions

During political interactions, you help others discover how to learn from the exchange and how to create new meaning. You accomplish this by breaking up complex ideas and tasks into smaller parts, asking questions, determining the extent of the understanding that occurs, and focusing learning on a specific goal or action. However, it should be stressed that you are instrumental in helping others reflect on their own understanding. Reflection is an intentional and complex activity during which other people address feelings associated with experiences, review and replay experiences, and reevaluate experiences in light of their awareness and feelings. Consequently, you are particularly effective if you are able to help others question their current assumptions, focus on new understanding, or overcome negative past experiences. This occurs by providing direction regarding people's patterns of thinking and unbiased advice. Effective political navigators allow and encourage others to assume responsibility for new understanding.

Questions for Improving Political Interaction

Certainly, improving political interactions is a challenging endeavor. You are better prepared for political interactions by addressing the following questions:

1. What is the need for the political interaction?
2. Who is participating in the political interaction?
3. What are the expectations and commitment of participants in the political interaction?
4. Do other key decision makers in the organization have an interest in this political interaction?
5. What is the scope of the political interaction?
6. Where will the political interaction take place?
7. What other groups (i.e., departments, units, divisions) may be affected by the political interaction?
8. What related political interactions have occurred in the past?
9. What were the results of the past political interaction?
10. What are the sources of support during the political interaction?
11. What are the possible constraints during the political interaction?
12. What other economic, political, or cultural factors may affect the success of the political interaction?

Outcome of a Political Interaction: Self-Esteeming

The primary outcome of a *positive* political interaction is known as self-esteeming. Self-esteeming can be defined as the mutual and reciprocal respect and confidence that ensue from two parties working collaboratively to achieve desired results. Self-esteem creates a condition where the whole is greater than the sum of the parts. It is based upon the enormously powerful need of people to feel good about themselves and their experiences. In short, self-esteeming is the sum total of how people feel about themselves as a result of a political interaction.

Self-esteeming is reciprocal where everyone benefits by working and interacting together. Political navigators interact with other people every day, which provides them numerous opportunities to enhance or diminish their self-esteem. These interactions may include one-on-one meetings, performance confrontations, delegating or observing work assignments or activities, discussions, presentations, proposals, and so forth. Together, these interactions constitute other people's "private and public world," a world they draw upon to bolster their self-esteem. On the other hand, this world can deplete self-esteem, particularly when political interactions are negative, which can result in feelings of depression, anger, or resentment.

Self-esteeming is a bit like a debit and credit account from which people draw to build up or diminish their self-concept. The balance within the account fluctuates based upon political interactions (i.e., experiences). Over time, political interactions produce a type of "net balance" of experiences—both positive and negative. For some, positive political interaction also gives them the confidence to take risks, grow, and be expressive, courageous, and self-assured. Positive interactions produce a positive self-concept, which enables people to feel comfortable with themselves. People with a positive self-concept are able to be and become whatever they desire. Conversely, individuals possessing a negative self-concept are often defensive, bitter, mistrusting, reclusive, frightened, critical, or resentful. When these attitudes prevail, people are not receptive to advice or feedback and are reluctant to take on new challenges. Their attitude toward conflict is often negative because it is perceived as an additional attack on their self-concept as opposed to an opportunity for growth and development.

Every political interaction is an opportunity to enhance or deplete another person's self-concept. For example, assigning work to employees is a political interaction that can both energize and keep employees engaged or diminish their self-concepts. Positive political interactions help others grow and develop, which encourages them to tackle increasingly difficult, challenging assignments or foster dependency and self-doubt.

Perhaps one of the major obstacles in becoming a political navigator is identifying ways of enhancing other people's self-esteem. Four primary sources contribute to enhancing people's self-esteem:

- achieving mastery and success
- obtaining power, command, control, and influence
- being appreciated and valued
- having their values and beliefs acknowledged

Each of these sources serves as a conduit for people's experiences (their world) to contribute to their overall self-esteem level. These four sources of self-esteem enable positive experiences to flow into a person's self-concept "bucket." The more positive experiences they have, the higher their self-esteem level will become. That is, the higher their self-esteem level, the greater their self-concept will be. Overtime, people's experiences either add to or subtract from their self-concept bucket, which either raises or lowers their level of self-esteem.

When people participate in a negative political interaction, it lowers their self-concept, producing negative attitudes and poor outcomes. People will not want to engage in future political interactions that may negatively impact their self-esteem. If this cycle is allowed to continue, the result is angry, resentful people who are fearful of engaging in important political interactions. Consequently, you must find ways of providing positive political interactions that help fill others' self-concept buckets, which can best be done by using one or all of the aforementioned four sources of self-esteem.

Identifying the Differences between Political Engagements and Political Interactions

A political interaction differs from a political engagement in the following ways. A political interaction is a one-on-one exchange with an individual or group for the purpose of gaining a distinctive advantage, building a relationship, sharing information, and/or identifying needs, interests, and expectations. Political interactions are designed to produce small-scale, micro results and outcomes and are proactive and partnership relationship oriented exchanges. They promote goodwill and a cooperative spirit. On the other hand, political engagements are designed to execute a plan and strategy for the purpose of achieving a large-scale macro results and outcomes (see chapter 6). They are full-scale aggressive actions. Typically, they are reactive and not designed to promote cooperation but to defend and protect you and things you value.

Political engagements are like military campaigns in that there are a large number of participants actively involved on both sides seeking to achieve different results and outcomes. On the other hand, political interactions are typically solitary exchanges where one person participates in an exchange with a few individuals or a small group. Further, political engagements have a series of phases that must be followed to guarantee success, while political interactions primarily rely on your ability to interact, communicate, and persuade other individuals to take action on your behalf. Finally, political engagements utilize the scientific method as the mechanism for execution but political interactions are free-form, process-oriented discussions that may or may not have a political objective or outcome other than maintaining one's credibility or building a better relationship.

UNDERSTANDING YOUR ORGANIZATION

It is helpful to liken organizations to icebergs: the formal components of the organization represent that part of the iceberg seen above the water, while the informal components lie beneath the water's surface—unseen, undetected, unknown, yet clearly an organizational element. The formal components are the publicly observable, structural elements that include the organization's span of control, mission, goals, objectives, procedures, policies, hierarchical levels, and practices. On the other hand, informal organizational components are not observable and consist of the informal power structure, patterns of intergroup and intragroup relationships, personal perceptions of the organization, openness, risk-taking behaviors, perceptions of trust, and individual relationships between managers and their employees.

Political navigators consider both the formal and informal organization. They understand that the scope and intensity of political problems will manifest themselves in the informal components of the organization. Political navigators also realize that true problem solving only occurs when the informal organization and all of its behaviors and practices are radically altered. The depth of political success is based on how willing the political navigator is to go deep into the organizational iceberg to solve a problem.

Political navigators demonstrate a thorough understanding of their organization. This requires a solid comprehension of business fundamentals so that you understand how organizations operate, how decisions are made, and how business gets done (see chapter 3). Demonstrating organizational understanding may require additional advance study in organizational psychology, communications, organizational development, and change management. Failure to actively improve your organizational knowledge, and thus credibility, may produce catastrophic effects.

Quite simply, organizational understanding is evident when you demonstrate an awareness of how things get done and who is essential in the execution of critical job functions useful in achieving business results. Acquiring such insight may require you to work closely with other people in different job classifications and/or participate in a job exchange program. Regardless of how you go about acquiring it, the insight into your organization's operations and human resource function you gain is invaluable.

UNDERSTANDING YOUR CLIENTS

Political success begins by identifying the individuals who have something to gain or lose as a result of a political interaction or engagement. These individuals are known as "clients." These include employees, other managers, organizational leaders, and sometimes the organization's customers. These individuals often have different perspectives of the organization, which are the result of varying experiences. Based on the quantity and quality of these experiences, clients draw vastly different conclusions. By identifying a client's perspective of the organization, you are better able to:

1. understand why clients behave the way they do;
2. identify clients' willingness to embrace your ideas and recommendations;
3. identify clients' deeply rooted assumptions and beliefs about the organization and its leadership;
4. predict a client's future behaviors and decisions;
5. identify a client's level of support and involvement when implementing your ideas and recommendations;
6. identify potential gatekeepers whose main purpose in the organization is to be obstructionists and maintainers of the status quo.

By doing these things, you are considering people that you interact with as clients. You recognize that there are different types of clients that have differing needs and expectations. Finally, you make every attempt to build collaborative relationships with your clients to meet their needs and expectations and to improve communications (see chapters 3 and 4).

Types of Clients

Although it may seem counterintuitive, one of the biggest mistakes you can make is treating all clients in the same way. Some clients have the power to make decisions and provide the financial and human resources needed to achieve results. Some can derail your efforts, while others can affect the outcome by altering other people's perceptions regarding a political situation. Certain clients can provide the technical advice needed to ensure the implementation of new ideas, while others are responsible for implementing political solutions. Still others guide the interaction between client groups and provide insight into the implementation of political solutions.

In any political interaction or engagement, there are four different types of clients, each of which has a distinct reason for participating. Political navigators understand and address each type of client. The client types include decision makers, stakeholders, influencers, and scouts

Decision Makers. Decision makers are most commonly the senior executives in the organization and they have the authority to give final approval for political solutions. They also have direct access to financial and human resources that can be used when implementing political solutions. Moreover, decision makers enjoy veto power that can prevent a solution from being implemented.

The primary focus of a decision maker is the bottom line and the impact a political solution will have on the organization. He or she is most interested in the return on investment that the organization will receive by implementing solutions. Political navigators can eliminate decision makers' concerns by answering their questions and providing evidence that supports their recommendations. The impact of any political solution must be clearly communicated. Impact can include increased profitability, enhanced revenue, or improved performance.

Stakeholders. Stakeholders are those individuals who have the most to gain or lose as a result of implementing a political solution. Stakeholders must implement and supervise a given solution; therefore, its impact on departments, units, and divisions within the organization must be evaluated. Stakeholders will have to "live" with the political solution; consequently, it becomes a very personal decision for which they will be held accountable.

To meet stakeholders' needs and expectations, you as a political navigator must reassure them that the solution will indeed help improve organizational outcomes. You communicate your intent during political solutions. This information will reassure stakeholders that you will help them implement complex political solutions as well as assist in overcoming other peoples' resistance to change.

Influencers. Many influencers view their role as that of screening political solutions deemed impractical or inappropriate for the organization. As a result, they serve as gatekeepers by changing the perceptions of decision makers and stakeholders regarding proposed solutions. In such situations, influencers do not have the authority to approve the selection of a political solution but can greatly impact the selection process.

Politically naïve managers avoid, discount, or minimize the impact of influencers, which is a serious mistake. One of the best ways of dealing with influencers is by validating them. This is done by soliciting their opinions, ideas, and assistance. Additionally, address the concerns of influencers with quantifiable, measurable evidence or by demonstrating how they benefit as a result of the proposed political solution. Such an approach will help elevate the influencer in the eyes of decision makers and stakeholders, which is precisely what influencers desire.

Scouts. In every political interaction and engagement, someone serves as a point person, acting as a guide during interactions with decision makers, stakeholders, and influencers, and yourself. They provide and interpret information about the problem, potential causes, client expectations, types of clients involved, and ways to proceed. Scouts may be found throughout the organization. They focus on the success of a political solution because they believe the solution will help improve organizational effectiveness. Consequently, most scouts serve as change ambassadors within the firm.

Credible scouts often have organizational insight and understanding that many managers may lack. They possess an awareness and intuition about what will or will not work within the organization and are conscious of how each decision maker, stakeholder, and influencer will benefit from a successful political solution. This insight is invaluable to you as you struggle to help the organization improve. Before you solicit the help of scouts, make certain that these individuals have credibility with other decision makers, stakeholders, and influencers. Once the scout's credibility has been established, you work closely with him or her, including soliciting and accepting advice from that person unless it seriously violates your professional values or ethics.

Identifying Clients' Needs and Expectations

It is impossible for a political navigator to achieve desired political results without identifying clients' needs and expectations. Needs are the problems or issues that must be resolved for people to reach their personal and professional goals and objectives. These include improved business results, better organizational communications, improved developmental strategies, and so on. Quite simply, they are the gaps that must be filled in order for people to function effectively and provide value in the organization. The following questions help identify client needs:

- What is the difference between the current and desired results?
- What are the needs of their customers, partners, and competitors?
- Who else must have input into meeting the needs of their customers, partners, and competitors?
- Am I able to meet these needs?

Next, political navigators identify which of the stated needs are most prevalent and design strategies to fulfill them.

Identifying expectations is an important way of understanding how clients meet personal and professional goals and objectives. However, all parties understand how expectations differ from needs. Expectations are outcomes desired by clients while needs are requirements that must be addressed for clients to maintain satisfactory performance. In other words, needs are the minimal or baseline requirements that must be met for the clients to succeed. Expectations are usually the benchmarks that clients hope to achieve. Client needs must be met and client expectations must be achieved if organizations are to maintain viability.

Expectations are the outcomes that individuals anticipate from a political interaction or engagement. Expectations are realistic and attainable when you establish clients' satisfaction levels. Additionally, expectations are those things that clients assume they will receive as a result of a positive political interaction or engagement. On the other hand, expectations may be set so high as to be unachievable. When this occurs, clients become melancholy and possibly mediocre, as they fail to see how their work is beneficial or contributory to positive organizational results.

UNDERSTANDING THE POLITICAL CLIMATE OF YOUR ORGANIZATION

An important ingredient of establishing credibility in an organization is to identify the type of political arena that exists. To do so, closely observe the interactions, conflicts, and behaviors of organizational members. From this activity, four political arenas emerge.

The first type of political environment is known as the *fairyland organization*. This type organization consists of atmospheres that are amicable in which conflict is rare if it ever occurs. In such organizations, competition among coworkers is discouraged and camaraderie is common. People treat each other with unconditional positive regard, are considerate, and do not often resort to heavy-handed politics.

The *team-oriented organization* is characterized by a set of well-understood rules and formalities from which employees operate. Conflicts are not uncommon, although they tend to be moderate. Further, unsanctioned means of achieving individual and group performance objectives and organizational goals are not unusual, although if detected, they would be denied as having taken place. This is because leaders in this type of organization prefer to covey the impression that everything is done by the rules. Organizations such as this suffer from a kind of schizophrenia in which they expect one thing (performance/behavior) and reward another.

The third type of political environment is known as the *competitive organization*. In this type of political environment, conflict is common because formally sanctioned rules are seldom invoked. People are commonly classified as part of an in-group or out-group, which creates an environment of the haves versus the have-nots. Few people have the opportunity to interact with executives and senior managers because reporting relationships are very formal and hierarchical. Thus, working in this type of organization is highly stressful and turnover is very common.

The *pathological organization* is the fourth type of political environment. These organizations are seldom productive because daily interaction is fractious. Moreover, most goals and objectives are achieved by going around the formal procedures of the organization and conflict is an everyday event. Accordingly, distrust is very high and people spend a great deal of their time watching their backs to avoid negative repercussions and reprisals.

CONCLUSION

Becoming a political navigator is a very difficult but rewarding endeavor. It requires you to recognize the symptoms of heavy-handed politics and to develop strategies for dealing with difficult people. As such, you develop an understanding of the art and science of the political interaction process and an understanding of your organization. Political navigators are able to differentiate among the different types of clients that engage in political interactions and engagements as well as identify strategies for addressing their needs and expectations. Finally, you need to develop a radar system for detecting the different types of political environments that exist and ways of functioning within each.

TWO

Understanding Power, Politics, and Influence in Organizations

The study of power, politics, and influence and its effects is critical to understanding how organizations operate. The terms *power* and *influence* are often used interchangeably in the management literature; however, there are subtle, yet important, differences between these terms. For example, if an employee accepts a work assignment from you, that employee has been influenced by you. Power represents the capability to get someone to do something; influence is the exercise of that capability.

Organizational politics can be defined as those actions taken within an organization to acquire, develop, and use power and other resources to obtain one's preferred outcome in a situation in which there is uncertainty (or lack of consensus) about choices. Organizational politics arise when different groups pursue differing goals, and/or goals are unclear or ambiguous. It also arises when organizational and individual effectiveness is difficult to assess or goal achievement is prevented due to environmental turbulence.

Organizational influence refers to your ability to acquire the needed power to achieve results within the organization. It also includes the ability to motivate others and to persuade them to engage in activities or produce results they would otherwise not produce. Organizational influence sometimes refers to your ability to resolve conflicts, enhance communications, and build collaborative, synergistic relationships.

To become a success political navigator, you need to develop an understanding of several critical components of organizational survival: (1) power, (2) power tactics, (3) political behavior, (4) political influence tactics, (5) political conflict, and (6) conflict management styles.

UNDERSTANDING POWER

Becoming an effective political navigator involves increasing your personal power, which enhances your position or provides you opportunities to make connections with individuals who can assist you in your quest for political influence. However, power can be perceived as negative when individuals become addicted to it and use it unnecessarily or without regard for the well-being of others. Further, it can be perceived as a negative because many people have experienced negative outcomes from those who occupy traditional positions of power (e.g., parents, teachers, principals, ministers, etc.).

Power, like influence, involves a relationship between two people. Power is interpersonal, not personal. Power is related to dependency. For example, person A is powerful if person B is dependent on resources controlled by A. Dependency is the key to power, and the greater B's dependency on A, the greater power A has over B. To reduce a person's power, decrease dependency on the resources controlled by that person.

Dependency is increased when the resources you control are important, scarce, and nonsubstitutable. *Important* refers to the criticality and value of a resource. *Scarce* refers to the availability of a resource, while *nonsubstitutable* refers to the nonviability of an alternative. Power is the ability to (potentially or actually) control other people and to impose your will on others.

Power is the ability of one person to affect the behavior of someone else in a desirable way. It is also the ability of a person or group to influence another person or group. Power is based on formal authority, knowledge, personality, and access to information. It is also based on a person's ability to control resources. Power is typically used to obtain a desired result. It is used to get others to perform a certain action that they normally would not perform. It is used to push a group to accomplish the goals of another person and to control other people. It is distributed both formally and informally and is used to get accomplished what the most powerful person wants. Finally, managers who understand power and its effects possess much greater autonomy than those who do not.

Power can sometimes become addictive and is not relinquished easily. However, power does not last forever, and transitions of power often result in major conflict in organizations. Consequently, you must have a complete understanding of who has power and how they use it in the organization.

Power is based on five elements. First, power is grounded formal authority, which is present in any reporting relationship. Second, power is based on knowledge: the more knowledge you possess, the more powerful you are. Third, power is based on personality. Individuals with persuasive, charismatic personalities typically are granted greater power. Fourth, power is based on one's ability to control information. Information is essential to decision-making, goal setting, and communications. Fifth, power is based on one's ability to control resources and increases as people become more dependent on the resources you control.

There are two perspectives on power: distributive and integrative. The distributive perspective is based on the philosophy that the amount of power is limited. In other words, the sum of power available for distribution is like a pie, so when a person acquires greater slice of power it is at the expense of others. Further, rights and interests of individuals are subordinate to power, and power is fought over, which leads to win-lose conflict. The distributive perspective of power relies on force, pressure, coerciveness, manipulation, and aggressiveness as means of getting things done. It is most common when people possess absolute power, such as emperors or dictators. Distributive power is centralized, limited to a few people, and is organized in a hierarchy.

The integrative perspective of power is based on joining forces, cooperation, collaboration, and problem solving. It is based on a philosophy that the pie can be expanded and shared. The rights and interest of individuals are given greater priority than power. The integrative view is most common when power is shared by others to get something accomplished, which allows movement towards a win-win outcome. Organizations that rely on several people to achieve a goal or use a number of experts will most likely use integrative power. The benefits of sharing power include improving communication, enhancing cooperation, and creating synergy.

Sources of Interpersonal Power

In 1959, John French and Bertram Raven identified five types of interpersonal power, each based on its source: expert, referent, legitimate, reward, and coercive. These sources of power are not equally available to all members of the organization. These sources of power can be defined as:

1. Expert power is due to special skill or knowledge.
2. Referent power depends on appeal, admiration, magnetism, identification, and charisma.
3. Legitimate power, usually called authority, flows from a person's position in the organization, which grants authority to command.
4. Reward power stems from the leader's ability to control rewards given to other people, who are perceived in a positive manner, and helps achieve desired outcomes.
5. Coercive power depends on the ability to execute threats, punish others, and create fear in an organization.

The expert and referent power are informal sources, while the last three are formal sources of power. It is helpful to recognize which type of power exists and associate each source with specific individuals within the organization. Accordingly, you can better prepare for political interactions and engagements by using the most appropriate source of power. This will maximize your influence, which is invaluable when building a guiding coalition responsible for implementing, facilitating, and managing change and evaluating political engagements. Finally, these five sources of power are directly parallel to the organizational chart in that the first two sources of power typically reside in employees with specific areas of expertise, while the last three typically reside in senior managers in the organization. Consequently, you should identify patterns and symbols for each source of power so that you can respond accordingly. Let's examine each of the sources of power more closely.

Expert Power. This power involves demonstrating the proficiency and aptitude necessary to perform a series of tasks or performance activities that others cannot. Individuals with expert power are given special status in a work group or organization and are excellent candidates when developing best practices, exploratory procedures, and efficiencies. Expert power is also afforded those who possess special skills or knowledge critical to organizational success. The bases of power and influence for experts are their advanced knowledge, the reservoir of information they possess, and the quality of their advice.

There are several ways that you can demonstrate your expert power more effectively in your organization. First, act confidently and decisively when others question your thoughts, ideas, and opinions. Second, remain informed and up-to-date through constant study and personal examination. Third, promote an image of expertise by appearing thoughtful and reflective, which can be facilitated by using the communication skills discussed in chapter 4. In addition, people who present themselves in a professional and polished manner have an easier time building positive relationships with others. This is why dressing for success and demonstrating proper etiquette is so critical to upward mobility. Therefore, the more you look and act the part of a competent professional, the more likely others will treat you that way. It is that simple.

Referent Power. This power is based on a personality or style of behavior marked by charisma and personal magnetism that easily attracts admiration and appeal. Accordingly, many people trust individuals with referent power and are influenced by their persuasive communication skills.

To demonstrate your referent power more effectively in your organization, you can do the following: First, treat subordinates fairly and defend their interests. Second, be sensitive to subordinates' needs, expectations, and feelings. Third, engage in role modeling activities whenever possible. This refers to demonstrating desired behaviors that are critical to achieving results in the organization.

Legitimate Power. This power is based on a person's ability to influence others by being in a more powerful position. This type of power is sometimes referred to as authority because it flows from a person's position in the organization. The bases of power for these individuals are their position and authority to command.

Subordinates perform a major role in the exercise of legitimate power. They comply if they perceive the use of power as legitimate. However, the organizational culture determines the limits of legitimate power.

Approaches you can take to demonstrate your legitimate power more effectively in your organization include the following: First, be cordial, polite, and confident when interacting with other people in the organization. Second, make appropriate requests that are clearly within your level of authority. Third, enforce compliance to rules and regulations that are violated by others in the organization. This will demonstrate your willingness to exercise your authority in a legitimate manner and will also communicate that all individuals will be treated fairly and consistently. Finally, always follow proper channels when exercising your legitimate power. Again, this will communicate that you are not attempting to circumvent the rules and regulations that everyone else must follow.

Reward Power. This power stems from the leader's ability to control rewards given to other people. This type of power is often used when legitimate power fails to achieve desired results. Further, if subordinates value the rewards or potential rewards, they will response positively, but if the opposite is true, this type of power rarely works. Reward power works best when employees know how they can achieve the rewards and have the opportunity to assess their performance and adjust their behavior accordingly.

The following are steps you can take to demonstrate your reward power more effectively in your organization. First, make certain that you verify compliance and accomplishments before issuing rewards. Second, offer rewards for desired actions and behaviors and make certain that you are rewarding the outcomes others desire. Third, offer only credible rewards valued by others so that they are positively received.

Coercive Power. This power is the ability to punish others and is the opposite of reward power. Some subordinates may comply because of fear, but threats and punishment are seldom effective over time. Of course, the bases of coercive power are fear, intimidation, threats, punishment, and the withholding of rewards.

To demonstrate your coercive power more effectively in your organization, you can proceed in the following ways: First, understand the situation and circumstances before acting. Second, give warning before punishing and make certain that subordinates are informed of rules, regulations, and consequences before administering penalties. Third, administer punishment consistently and uniformly to all individuals in the organization. Finally, punish in private so that you do not embarrass others, which can seriously damage their self-esteem.

In organizations, power is typically used to obtain *commitment*, secure *compliance*, or overcome *resistance*. Therefore, it is important that you understand which source of power is most appropriate in achieving each of these desired outcomes. When obtaining commitment, it is best to rely on your expert and referent power, while it is most appropriate to use legitimate and reward power to increase compliance. Overcoming resistance can best be achieved by using coercive and legitimate power, but some believe that working with people in a consultative manner, demonstrating respect, and soliciting their opinions is the most effective way of mitigating resistance. Accordingly, you are using a new source of power by relying on your expertise as a political navigator as well as your ability to influence others, which is a form of referent power. In other words, overcoming resistance can best be achieved by adopting the skills of a political navigator and applying them appropriately and effectively (see chapter 4).

Other Sources of Power. There are a number of other sources of power that political navigators can rely on in achieving desired results. Three of the most common are: structural, decision-making, and information.

The structure of an organization often determines power relationships. Organizational structure creates a formal power and authority by specifying certain individuals to perform critical tasks and certain prescribed decisions. Additionally, structure significantly impacts informal power through its effects on information and communication flows within the firm.

Decision-making power is most common when an individual can control each step of the decision-making process. Such individuals have the ability to influence other peoples' decisions. They are known as power brokers and have influence over many people, regardless of their own position in the organization. Sometimes these individuals have the power to decide which decisions will be given priority and when those decisions are made.

Information power refers to one's access to relevant and important information. For example, accountants have access to important information that is often critical in making effective decisions. Generally, accountants do not have a particularly strong or apparent legitimate power base in the organization. Because they possess important information needed in making critical decisions, they have significant power.

In *The Secret Handshake* (2000), Kathleen Kelly Reardon outlines several other sources of power:

1. The *power of relevance* involves developing power based on what people do within the organization, linking their jobs, positions, and skills to the priorities of the organization.
2. The *power of centrality* involves receiving power that accrues from holding central positions in important networks, such as senior management planning teams, strategic planning committees, and reporting relationships to important executives and senior managers.
3. The *power of high confidence* involves being at ease under extremely stressful conditions.
4. The *power of autonomy* is evident when individuals are granted a degree of freedom, discretion, and independence to exercise the duties of their current position; thus, positions with the most autonomy have the most power.
5. The *power of career cachet* derives from holding a respected occupation in an organization. Those positions that are positively perceived are considered essential while others are not.
6. The *power of dedication* is granted to individuals who demonstrate long-term tenure or commitment to an organization. These individuals possess an understanding of the importance of institutional history and extensive organizational memory.
7. The *power of objectivity* is common among individuals who have been in their organizations a short while (less than two years), because they offer a unique source of power—objectivity. Such individuals provide an unbiased perspective about the organization and its policies, procedures, and culture.
8. The *power of positive impression* involves demonstrating an appearance that convinces others that you belong in positions of formal power.

As a political navigator, you can utilize each of these sources of power in your daily interactions, which will elevate you within the organization. As a result, you will make significant political gains within the organization.

UNDERSTANDING POWER TACTICS

Becoming a political navigator requires you to determine *who has the power* in your organization. Typically, people who can control and approve expenditures beyond the budget have substantial power in an organization. People who can intercede favorably on behalf of others and have the ability to get items on agendas at major meetings also possess significant power. As we discussed previously, people who control critical resources possess significant power. Finally, people who can get fast access to top decision makers in the organization are considered powerful.

People who control critical information, lines of communications, and decision criteria are very powerful. People who can select consultants or outside experts are also extremely powerful. Finally, people who can outline the goals, mission, and strategy of an organization as well as form networks, build coalitions, and negotiate and resolve conflict are among the most powerful in an organization.

Power Tactics

Two types of power tactics exist in organization: upward and downward. Upward power tactics referred to those techniques used when persuading a superior to accept a new idea (political solution). Under this circumstance, the most useful technique is to employ reason and logic to communicate the positive outcomes that will occur when implementing a new idea. It is often helpful to communicate that a "collective coalition" of people are in support of the new idea. This demonstrates that there is a great deal of support for the idea.

Downward power tactics are most often used when interacting with subordinates. Accordingly, the most effective techniques include reason, assertiveness, and threats of sanction because such techniques demonstrate both logic and determination. An underutilized but very effective technique is to demonstrate respect, sincerity, and friendliness toward subordinates. In this way, subordinates feel valued and respected and are more willing to accept suggestions and recommendations.

UNDERSTANDING POLITICAL BEHAVIOR

Becoming a political navigator requires you to understand why political behavior occurs within organizations. The primary reason that negative political behavior exists is a fear of uncertainty: people resist many good ideas, suggestions, recommendations, and changes because of fear of the unknown. Negative political behavior also exists because of a perceived threat from managers and the organization. This could include fear of demotions, layoffs, relocations, and reassignments.

Another reason negative political behavior exists is ambiguous goals and objectives in the organization. When this occurs, individuals are uncertain whom to follow and why. Ambiguous goals cause people to spend an inordinate amount of time on activities that may not be perceived as important by organizational leaders. Consequently, their efforts are not valued, and over time, this can create uncertainty, resentment, and discontentment.

Negative political behavior is also common when one's position and authority are uncertain. This sometimes occurs when organizations are going through restructuring, mergers, and acquisitions. Furthermore, the erosion of one's position and authority can have a negative affect on one's self-esteem and confidence.

Sometimes uncertainties in the external environment, technological advancements, and innovations can create negative political behavior. This is most common during periods of recession or expansion in which individuals' jobs are at risk. Consequently, people are less willing to take risks, which can severely impact innovation and creative problem solving.

Negative political behavior occurs during periods of organizational change. This is because peoples' worlds, as they know them, have changed forever. Under such circumstances, many people are reluctant to support change and even sabotage, undercut, and circumvent it.

There are many factors that influence political behavior. They can be clustered into two categories: individual and organizational factors. The political behavior of individuals is often controlled by their investment in the organization, perception of job alternatives (internal and external), expectations of success in the organization, internal locus of control, and self-motivation. Organizational factors that affect political behavior include reallocation of resources, promotional opportunities for employees, role ambiguity, performance criteria, and low trust. Other factors include self-serving senior managers and organizational leaders, high performance pressure, and ambiguous and uncertain compensation and reward criteria. Political behavior can be positively or negatively affected by each of these individual and organizational factors.

Understanding Defensive Political Behaviors

Becoming a political navigator requires you to understand defensive political behaviors and develop strategies for avoiding, overcoming, and/or dealing with them. The effects of defensive political behaviors include slowing down decision-making, increasing interpersonal and intragroup

tension, and restricting change. If left unchecked, defensive political behaviors can lead to organizational rigidity and stagnation, organizational
cultures that are highly politicized, and detachment of individuals from
the organization's environment.

There are some common defensive political behaviors demonstrated
by people. They include avoiding action, blame, and change. Common
behaviors for *avoiding action* include:

- Overconforming—following the rules precisely
- Passing the buck—"that is somebody else's responsibility"
- Playing dumb—"I don't know"
- Depersonalization—treating people as objects or numbers
- Stretching—prolonging an existing task: "I'm too busy"
- Smoothing—covering up fluctuations in effort
- Stalling—foot dragging

Common behaviors for *avoiding blame* include:

- Formalizing—documenting one's every move
- Playing it safe—only taking tasks with high probability of success
- Justifying—developing explanations that lessen one's own responsi-
  bility
- Scapegoating—placing blame on external factors or others
- Misrepresenting—selective presentation and distortion of informa-
  tion
- Escalation of commitment—showing others that you still believe it
  was a good idea ("throwing good money after bad")

Finally, common behaviors for *avoiding change* include resisting change
(stalling, playing safe, misrepresenting, and so on) and protecting turf
("this is our responsibility, not yours").

UNDERSTANDING POLITICAL INFLUENCE TACTICS

It could be said that influence is what playing politics is all about. In
fact, individuals and people engage in political behavior as a way of influencing the perceptions or behaviors of other individuals and groups.
Accordingly, there are specific tactics used to influence individuals within
the organization. Cecilia M. Falbe and Gary A. Yukl identified nine influence tactics in their classic article published in the *Journal of Applied Psychology* in 1990.

1. Inspirational appeals—making emotional requests that appeal to people's feelings and values or increase others' confidence that the desired course of action will be successful
2. Consultation—seeking advice or participation in planning or decision-making, which is used to support your efforts, positions, or course of action
3. Personal appeals—using feelings of loyalty and friendship, as well as relationships, to gain support for your efforts, positions, or course of action
4. Exchange—negotiating cooperation to gain support by promising that others will receive a reward or benefit if they support your efforts, positions, or course of action
5. Integration—doing nice things voluntarily for others now with the expectation that in the future they will feel they owe you something in return
6. Rational persuasion—convincing others that your efforts, positions, or course of action is more logical; they will be better off under your approach
7. Coalition—forming a group of allies who have common interests in your efforts, positions, or course of action
8. Pressure tactics—using demands, intimidation, or threats to gain support for your efforts, positions, or course of action
9. Legitimizing—asking higher authorities to convince others to support your efforts, positions, or course of action

Each of these influence tactics can lead to several outcomes. The three most common include commitment, compliance, and resistance. Commitment involves people's willingness to support decisions, actions, or requests enthusiastically. Compliance occurs when individuals are willing to support your efforts, positions, or course of action but do so in an unenthusiastic manner. Resistance occurs when people openly oppose your efforts, positions, or course of action and try to avoid doing or supporting them.

In 1992, Cecilia M. Falbe and Gary Yukl conducted a study of over 500 individuals using the previously discussed influence tactics to determine their effects on the three previously discussed outcomes (commitment, compliance, and resistance). Interestingly enough, inspiration (90%), consultation (55%), personal appeals (42%), exchange (35%), and integration (31%) had the greatest affect on people's willingness to make commitments to a course of action. Coalition (3%), pressure (3%), and legitimizing (0%) had virtually no effect on people's commitment to a course of action. However, they were the three most identified influence tactics used in dealing with resistance and achieving compliance to a course of action. It could be concluded that differing influence tactics should be use based on your desired outcome. In summary, you should use inspirational appeals, consultation, and personal appeals to obtain commitment to your efforts, positions, or course of action and use coalition, pressure, and legitimizing tactics when overcoming resistance and seeking compliance.

UNDERSTANDING POLITICAL CONFLICT

Conflict can be defined as a process in which one person perceives that his or her interests are being imposed on or negatively affected by another. Conflicts can be a very difficult to resolve because of the emotional baggage that people possess as a result of previous experiences. It is, however, helpful to consider conflict as an opportunity because it provides you a mechanism for identifying a variety of possible solutions to problem. Moreover, conflict can be viewed as a journey that allows you to pursue common ground for the negotiating parties. Finally, conflict can be viewed as "war for resources and influence," in that there is a clear winner and loser.

Becoming a political navigator requires you to distinguish between functional conflict and dysfunctional conflict. Quite simply, functional conflict serves an organization's interests while dysfunctional conflict threatens it. A functional conflict is a confrontation between individuals and groups that enhances and benefits the organization. It allows people the opportunity to discuss the issues from a variety of vantage points. At the conclusion of such discussions, people have a better understanding of the situation, alternatives, potential solutions, and possible interventions that can be used to resolve the problem. These ingredients help to identify the best possible alternative(s) and solution(s) to the problem. Additional benefits of such discussions include stronger relationships, fair and equitable agreements, and greater self-awareness and creative problem solving.

A dysfunctional conflict is any confrontation or interaction between individuals and groups that harms the organization or hinders the achievement of its goals and objectives. Such conflict should be aggressively eliminated because it creates stress that is destructive and counterproductive.

Some people mistakenly approach conflict resolution as simply a disagreement over an issue or issues. While a disagreement may be the reason that people are at an impasse, there is a variety of other factors, conditions, and elements that impact the situation. For example, unresolved issues from the past can greatly influence a person's objectivity and rationality. People may be harboring bad feelings toward others, their department, or the organization as a whole. There may be hidden agendas or expectations that block or prevent open, honest, and direct discussion of the issue. The self-perceptions and self-esteem of all parties involved may negatively impact the situation. The interests, needs, and desires of all parties may also negatively impact the situation. Finally, the emotions and personalities of all parties may further cloud the discussions and negatively impact resolution of the problem. Ultimately these factors can negatively affect the resolution of the problem and can extend the negotiations indefinitely. Consequently, you need to examine all of these variables as possible contributors and develop strategies for addressing each. Otherwise, prepare for protracted negotiations and possibly an unresolved situation.

UNDERSTANDING CONFLICT MANAGEMENT STYLES

Differences between people are a major source of interpersonal tension and are the primary reason for much misunderstanding and conflict. People communicate, manage stress, handle emotions, and deal with conflicting opinions differently. Some are very task oriented, while others are very sensitive to the feelings of others. These differences are not necessarily a bad thing; however, they can lead to misunderstanding, resentment, and conflict that should be minimized as much as possible. Because people are important to your success as a political navigator, it is important to discover why people think, make decisions, and use time differently than you.

Foundations of the Conflict Management Style Model

Workplace management models are based on the research, insights, and experience of others. The conflict management style model is no exception. In the 1970s, two major Midwestern universities (Ohio State University and the University of Michigan) conducted a series of leadership studies examining the dimensions of leadership style. A series of studies at Ohio State University indicated that two behavioral dimensions prove significant in successful leadership:

- Consideration: mutual trust, respect, warmth, and behavior indicative of friendship
- Initiating structure: the establishment of well-defined patterns of organization, channels of communication, ways of getting jobs done, and behavior that organizes and defines relationships or role

The University of Michigan studies revealed similar concepts of leadership style that correlated with effectiveness:

- Employee orientation: human relations aspects of the leader's job, with the employees considered as human beings of intrinsic importance, individuality, and personal needs
- Production orientation: stress on production and technical aspects of the job, with employees viewed as a means of getting the work done

These are quite similar conceptualizations and reveal that successful leaders (success is defined in terms of productivity and employee satisfaction) engage in both behaviors in varying degrees and not in one or the other dimensions exclusively. Therefore, leaders must behave in a manner consistent with task orientation and also a manner consistent with relationship orientation.

In 1985, Robert Blake and Jane Mouton developed a two-dimensional grid known as the Managerial Grid. It focused on task and relationship orientations uncovered in the Ohio State University and the University of Michigan leadership behavior studies. The principal difference in Blake and Mouton's model is that they did not demonstrate leadership choices as points on a continuum but created a grid based on managers' concerns for both people (relationships) and production (task). This working model showed each of these concerns as one of two axes of a grid, so concerns for both people and productivity combine in various management styles. Their model identified four different types of management style representing these two dimensions:

- team leader—high task, high people oriented
- authoritarian—high task, low people oriented
- country club—low task, high people oriented
- impoverished manager—low task, low people oriented

Conflict Management Style Model. The conflict management style model is adapted from these earlier leadership and management models, but its focus is conflict management style. It is useful because in most conflict situations you have little time to analyze another person's behavior and make adjustment. Therefore, I believe that the most useful way to help you identify another's conflict management style is through observation. The genius of the conflict management styles method is that it requires you to focus on just two dimensions of behavior. Only two! Out of the multitude of signals given by another person, you only have to observe two clusters of behavior to ascertain that person's conflict management style.

In Figure 2.1, two orientations are identified: *results-outcomes* (meaning task or production orientation) and *responsiveness* (meaning employee/relationship orientation). These two dominions are very helpful in predicting how people are likely to behave during conflict. These key dimensions of behavior combine to form the Conflict Management Style Model.

Conflict situations are those in which two or more people appear to be incompatible. In such situations, people's behavior falls along two basic dimensions:

1. results-outcomes orientation—the extent to which a person attempts to achieve a desired result or outcome
2. responsiveness to people's needs and expectations—the extent to which a person attempts to meet the needs and expectations of others

These two basic dimensions of behavior can be fully defined in five specific styles of dealing with conflict or conflict handling modes.

It is useful to think of the results-outcomes axis as a continuum in which a person's conflict management behavior is typically more results-

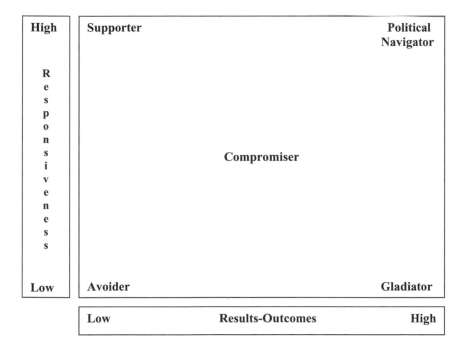

Figure 2.1. Conflict Management Styles

outcomes oriented or less results-outcomes oriented than that of half the population. People whose characteristic conflict management behavior is more results-outcomes oriented than half of the population are sometimes referred to as being on the *right side* of the continuum. People on the *left side* of the continuum get their needs met by using a less forceful and less directive manner and are considered less results-outcomes oriented half of the population.

Some mistakenly believe that submissive behavior is attributed to those individuals in the lower levels of results-outcomes orientations, which is simply not true. While some less results-outcomes oriented people are submissive, many simply use less forceful ways to get their needs met. What you need to focus on is whether a person's behavior *appears* less forceful and directive than it does for half the population. Further, results-outcomes orientation is not an indication of a person's inner drive, ambition, or motivation but is simply a reflection of how a person seeks to achieve results and outcomes.

It is useful to think of a continuum of responsiveness in which a person's behavior is typically more responsive or less responsive than that of half the population. People whose characteristic behavior is more responsive than that of half the population are sometimes referred to as being at the *top* of the continuum, while people on the *bottom* of the continuum are considered less responsive than half of the population.

Five Conflict Management Styles. Each person's conflict management style is a unique blend of two dimensions: results-outcomes orientation and responsiveness to people's needs and expectations (Figure 2.1). Nevertheless, most people fall more or less into one or another of the five styles known as: *supporter, avoider, gladiator, compromiser,* and *political navigator.*

Supporters are highly responsive to the concerns of people and non-results-outcomes oriented, a supporter is the opposite of a gladiator. Supporters are people oriented, friendly, accepting, cooperative, like to be liked, and are motivated to help others in a team effort. In the conflict situation, they spend little of their time attempting to achieve a desired result. Their primary concern is maintaining positive relationships with the people involved. Supporters neglect their own concerns to satisfy the concerns of other people. There's an element of self-sacrifice in this style.

During conflict, supporters give in completely to the other side with little or no attention to their own interests. Supporters play down the differences between themselves and others while emphasizing commonalities. The primary strength of this style is that it encourages cooperation, while its primary weakness is that it is a temporary fix that fails to confront the underlying problem.

The supporter style is appropriate when people are more important than achieving a specific outcome. It is also appropriate when the issue is much more important to another person than it is to you. Therefore, to satisfy the needs of others, you support their conclusions and recommendations, which helps maintain a collaborative working relationship. This style is also used to build up social credits for later issues or when continued competition will only damage the relationship you have with other people. The supporter style is also appropriate when you are outmatched and there is a high degree of certainty that you will lose and when preserving harmony and avoiding disruption are particularly important.

Avoiders are low in responsiveness to others and low in concern for results-outcomes and are the opposite of political navigators. Avoiders try to smooth things over or avoid conflict situations altogether. They make little or no effort to achieve a desired result-outcome nor are they concerned with the needs and expectations of other people. They do not pursue their own goals or those of other people. They do not address the conflict and conveniently sidestep the issue completely. They would prefer to postpone decisions and often withdraw from the situation altogether. Their tactics may include passive withdrawal from the problem or active suppression of the issue. The main strength of this style is that it buys time in unclear, unfolding, or ambiguous situations, while its primary weakness is that while it provides a temporary fix, it postpones addressing the underlying problems.

Avoidance is appropriate when the potential damage of confronting a conflict outweighs the benefits of resolving the conflict. The avoider style is also appropriate when the conflict is trivial or of only passing importance, and/or when other important issues are pressing. This approach is also valid when you perceive that there is no chance of satisfying your concerns over those of other people. Avoidance is beneficial when people need to cool down in order to reduce tensions so that they can remain objective and composed. When gathering more information outweighs the advantages of an immediate decision, the avoider style is suitable.

Gladiators are very results-outcomes oriented and nonresponsive to the concerns of other people. In other words, gladiators have a high concern for the issues important to them but have little concern for others, which encourages "I win, you lose" tactics. Gladiators pursue their own concerns at the expense of others. As with the gladiators of ancient times, this style strongly believes that they must win at all costs. They will pursue whatever means necessary to achieve the results they desire and have a little or no concern for future relationships, opportunities, and partnerships with other people.

Gladiators are goal-oriented, disciplined, determined "bottom-line" thinkers who push for results and accomplishments. Gladiators like control and rely on formal authority to force compliance. Speed is the gladiator style's primary strength, while its primary weakness is that its dominating tactics often breed resentment.

The gladiator style is most appropriate when important issues are being examined where you are certain you are right, and where the benefits of achieving the desired result or outcome outweigh the drawbacks that emerge from other people's negative feelings. This style is most appropriate when quick, decisive action is critical (emergencies) and for implementing unpopular courses of action (cost-cutting, discipline, layoffs). The gladiator style is essential on issues vital to the organization's welfare when there's a clear right answer. Finally, the gladiator style is appropriate when protecting yourself from people who take advantage of you or when results are counterproductive to the organization.

Compromisers are moderately results-outcomes oriented and moderately responsive to the concerns of other people. The primary goal of compromisers is to find an expedient, mutually acceptable solution that satisfies all parties. Compromisers give up more than gladiators but less than supporters when negotiating a solution to a conflict. They address issues more directly than avoiders but do not explore them as much as political navigators.

This is a give-and-take approach involving moderate but equal concerns for both people and results-outcomes. When two parties have opposite goals or possess equal power, compromise is appropriate. A primary strength of this style is that the democratic process has no losers; however, it is a temporary fix that can stifle creative problem solving and create further conflict in the future. Consequently, conflicts may arise again because the issues were not resolved adequately.

Compromisers seek the middle ground and strongly believe that any solution that resolves the immediate conflict is acceptable regardless of the long-term consequences. It is a good backup style when other approaches (mainly gladiator and supporter) fail to resolve the issue. The compromiser style is appropriate when two opponents with equal power are strongly committed to mutually exclusive goals. Further, this style is useful in achieving temporary settlements to complex issues and for arriving at expedient solutions under time pressure.

Political navigators are very results-outcomes oriented and highly responsive to people's needs and expectations. Political navigators are individualists; ones who believe in getting ahead by playing political games in a skillful, unobtrusive manner. They are not in the habit of using politics to advance personal objectives or personal agendas. They do not look for ulterior motives in others and have little regard for sanctioned rules. They are sometimes considered "smooth operators." Political navigators attempt to work with other people to find solutions that fully achieve the results-outcomes for all parties while maintaining positive relationships. They are willing to discuss issues completely in order to identify underlying concerns as well as identify alternatives that meet the needs and expectations of all parties. Finally, political navigators are skillful negotiators and are capable of demonstrating all of the skills and knowledge discussed in chapter 4.

Political navigators rely on their relationship building, communication, and conflict resolution skills to confront issues and cooperatively identify problems, generate and weigh alternative solutions, and select a solution. It could be said that political navigators use an integrative approach to solving complex issues plagued by misunderstandings, self-serving behavior, and dogmatic focus on inappropriate results and outcomes. The primary strength of this style is that the solutions identified and implemented are long-lasting in nature because they address the underlying political conflict rather than merely its symptoms. The primary weakness of this style is that it is very time-consuming and labor-intensive. Further, this style requires mastery of people skills and the facilitation of a rather sophisticated political engagement process (see chapter 6).

The political navigator style is most effective when working through hard feelings that have been exacerbated during periods of conflict. It is a useful style when it is important to find an integrated solution to a conflict while maintaining positive working relationships and when gaining commitment to resolution is critical. It could be said that the political navigator style is most useful when maintaining positive working relationships is as important as achieving desired results-outcomes. Of course, the opposite could apply. In other words, the political navigator style is most useful when achieving desired results-outcomes is as important as maintaining positive working relationships. In the final analysis, the political navigator style is desirous when conflict has become dysfunctional and a sophisticated, composed, and articulate approach is needed.

CONCLUSION

Becoming an effective political navigator requires you to develop a thorough understanding of power, power tactics, political behavior, political influence tactics, political conflict, and conflict management styles. Armed with this knowledge, you will be better prepared to address issues that create conflict in an organization. These insights also provide you adequate front wheel and back wheel expertise useful in becoming a politically savvy individual.

REFERENCES

Blake, Robert R., and Jane S. Mouton. *The Managerial Grid III: The Key to Leadership Excellence.* Houston: Gulf Publishing Co., 1985.

Falbe, Cecilia M., and Gary Yukl. "Consequences for Managers of Using Single Influence Tactics and Combinations of Tactics." *Academy of Management Journal* no. 3 (1992): 647.

French, John R. P., and Bertram H. Raven. "The Bases of Social Power." In *Studies of Social Power,* ed. D. Cartwright. Ann Arbor, MI: Institute for Social Research, 1959.

Reardon, Kathleen Kelly. *The Secret Handshake: Mastering the Politics of the Business Inner Circle.* New York: Doubleday, 2001.

Yukl, Gary, and Cecilia M. Falbe. "Influence Tactics and Objectives in Upward, Downward, and Lateral Influence Attempts." *Journal of Applied Psychology* 75, no. 3 (1990): 133.

THREE

Political Navigators' Roles and Responsibilities

Establishing credibility within the organization is the most important step in becoming a political navigator. Improved credibility results from your ability to understand your organization's operations and culture and demonstrate professional expertise. As a result, you are able to provide real value to the organization.

As a political navigator, you demonstrate several behaviors that enhance your credibility. First, you are predictable and consistent—dependable and reliable so that decision makers have confidence in your actions and recommendations. Second, you establish collaborative relationships built on trust and honesty. Third, you are accurate in all your practices as a manager. This includes performance appraisals, goal-setting activities, needs assessments, supervisory practices, problem solving, conflict resolution, recruiting and selection, job design, budgeting activities, motivation engagement, and performance coaching activities. Fourth, you meet your commitments in a timely and efficient manner. Fifth, you express your opinions, ideas, recommendations, and suggestions in an understandable and clear manner, and at the most appropriate times. Sixth, you demonstrate creativity and innovation. Seventh, you maintain confidentiality. Eighth, you behave in an ethical manner that demonstrates integrity.

Ninth, you listen to and focus on others problems in a manner that brings about mutual respect.

ROLES OF A POLITICAL NAVIGATOR

Credibility can also be established through an appropriate understanding and execution of differing roles. Such roles enable you to demonstrate your expertise in managing resources (time, energy, money, human talent, materials, equipment, and environment) and creating structures, systems, and processes that improve business results. Further, you can demonstrate your expertise by improving strategic decision making, improving employee relationships, resolving conflict, and building partnerships. When appropriate roles are executed, trust and confidence emerge, which deepens relationships and bridges performance uncertainty. Over time, improved efficiency results as collaboration and cooperation replace competition and conflict. The roles that enhance your credibility include: relationship builder, assertive communicator, negotiator, organizational expert, and partnership builder.

As previously stated, to improve credibility, you need to develop two types of competencies: professional expertise and political skills. To illustrate this concept, I asked you to visualize a bicycle, which has a front and back wheel. Front wheel competencies are essential when engaging in the relationship builder and assertive communicator roles. On the other hand, you demonstrate your back wheel competencies when you participate as an organizational expert. When you serve as a negotiator and partnership builder, you must possess both front and back wheel competencies (Figure 3.1).

Relationship Builder

A cornerstone role of the political navigator is that of relationship builder. This role requires you to build collaborative relationships with others that help you allocate resources, make decisions, and provide recommendations that improve organizational effectiveness. As such, demonstrate relationship skills such as listening, reflecting, questioning, and summarizing. Such skills build mutual acceptance and positive regard with people (see chapter 4). They also promote rapport and enhance your credibility so people will be willing to accept your recommendations during political interactions and engagements. This is clearly a "front wheel" role that is crucial to your success as a political navigator.

As a relationship builder, you develop a proper sharing environment. Relationship builders become personally involved with other people for

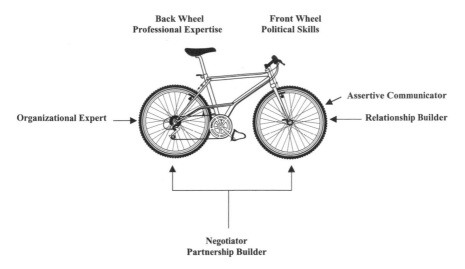

Figure 3.1. Front and Back Wheel Expertise and Skills and Political Navigator Roles

the purpose of improving the relationships and achieving a desired end. This does not mean that you overstep the personal boundaries established by the organization, but, rather, you engage in conversations that allow you to create a personal bond with others. Creation of personal bonds is essential to your success and includes the following elements: acceptance, involvement, attentiveness, empathy, genuineness, and, understanding.

Acceptance. Acceptance is the basic attitude that you hold toward other people. It requires respect for others as being persons of worth. You demonstrate acceptance through your willingness to allow people to differ from one another, which is based on the belief that each individual is a complex human being comprised of different experiences, values, and attitudes. As Carl Rogers (1961) stated in his classic work *On Becoming a Person,* "by acceptance I mean a warm regard for him/her as a person of unconditional self-worth ... an acceptance of and a regard for his/her attitudes ... no matter how negative or positive."

Involvement. Acceptance is a prerequisite to personal involvement, which requires you to spend significant time with another person. Without this involvement, you will never be able to develop the type of synergy that improves your political position within your organization. Involvement also includes willingness to care and feel responsible for other people. It implies action; it means active participation in people's problems and needs. During a political interaction, you become an active participant engaging in activities that allow face-to-face contact with other people. Maintaining good records of the outcomes of a political interaction also demonstrates your interest in others, which improves rapport.

One way of demonstrating involvement is through self-disclosure. This requires you to open up, sharing information both personal and professional, and reveals to others that you are a real human being with feelings and emotions. In short, self-disclosures demonstrate that you are a compassionate, feeling person. Second, you create personal involvement through observation. In fact, any workstation provides clues as to what is important to another person. Clues could include pictures of children, spouses, pets, and outdoor activities with friends; objects of affection; awards; and favorite books. You can discover a wealth of information with little or no effort.

Another type of observation technique is known as *relationship analysis*. This technique helps you discover a great deal about others' social patterns and relationships. Relationship analysis identifies people's socialization pattern and how this pattern is used in the workplace. The primary purpose of relationship analysis is to simply identify another person's relationship pattern so that you can better understand their personality, relationships, and interpersonal communication style. You are not judging or evaluating the social pattern, you are simply observing and attempting to understand it.

Conducting relationship analysis involves simply watching and observing others' interactions on a daily basis. These interactions reveal a great deal about peoples' values and beliefs, because people seldom spend time with those they feel uncomfortable with. As a result, you discover whom people feel comfortable with, whom they may desire to work with on future job assignments, and whom they consider colleagues and friends. Finally, relationship analysis allows you to identify the political connections people utilize in the workplace.

Political navigators can improve their personal involvement by asking questions that help them discover unique and interesting things about other people. Most people like talking about themselves, so let them. Thus, you take every opportunity to discover important events that occur in people's lives as well as uncover the things that hold personal meaning to them. People like it when others take a personal interest in them as human beings instead of viewing them only as employees of the organization.

Attentiveness. Attentiveness refers to the effort made by you to hear the message conveyed by another person. It requires skills in listening and observing. Ineffective managers cannot wait until others stop speaking so that they can present their own point of view. This communicates a lack of respect and diminishes the importance of others' ideas. On the other hand, listening conveys that you are interested in and sensitive to the feelings and thoughts of others.

A commonly used technique for demonstrating attentiveness is nonverbal communication. A simple nonverbal technique such as proper eye contact and nods of the head can greatly improve the communication between you and another person. Further, nonverbal communications is important in establishing and maintaining an environment that is conducive to sharing. Most people are quite aware of the nonverbal behavior of some managers and often avoid certain topics and discussions as a result. In fact, this might even lead a person to avoid interaction with senior managers, which certainly reduces their political effectiveness.

Empathy. You are considered empathetic when you have the ability to feel and describe the thoughts and feelings of others. Most typically, empathy is described as putting yourself in the other person's shoes, attempting, in other words, to see things from another person's vantage point. More importantly, empathetic understanding is the ability to recognize and understand the feelings that another person communicates through his or her behavioral and verbal expressions and to accurately communicate this understanding to that person. It is not enough to understand the behavior or feelings of other people; you must also communicate that understanding to them. True empathy is an active event rather than a passive one.

Genuineness. Genuineness implies being honest and candid with yourself while functioning as a political navigator and not pretending to be something you are not. It refers to your ability to be yourself in all situations, rather than play a part or role. It is demonstrated when you know your true feelings, act on them, and communicate them when appropriate. Genuineness implies self-disclosure, but does not mean you totally unveil your personal and private life. People want to believe in you. Honesty and candor provide the atmosphere for this to take place.

Understanding. Although no one fully understands another person, it can be said that the path to understanding is essentially a process of sharing. Understanding is demonstrated when you recognize and correctly interpret the feelings, thinking, and behavior of another person. People express themselves through verbal and nonverbal language that you attempt to interpret and put into words to clarify it for both of them.

Understanding can be characterized as internal and external. Internal understanding refers to your ability to step into the perceptual world of another person. This is done in an effort to discover their internal world—their fears, successes, and failures. It is at this level that genuine communication begins. External understanding refers to an awareness of another person's behavior and actions. This means being able to identify the actions of another person.

Assertive Communicator

Another important role of a political navigator is that of *assertive communicator*. This "front wheel" role is useful in developing and maintaining the interpersonal strategies necessary for creating long-lasting people relationships. It is impossible to interact with another person without confronting their ideas, beliefs, opinions, or positions. How can this be done and still maintain a positive collaborative relationship? It certainly cannot be accomplished through the aggressive, rude, abusive, or sarcastic tactics used by some managers, which are used to dominate others and attempt to force changes in their ideas, beliefs, opinions, or positions. In fact, these methods only create resentment and seldom help resolve differences.

Avoiding differences and pretending they do not exist cannot achieve positive collaborative relationships. While a submissive approach does not produce a direct confrontation, which can cause resentment and anger, it only postpones dealing with differences at a later date. Eventually differences must be addressed—typically when a relationship has deteriorated to such a point that drastic action must be taken. Often such action makes the situation even worse.

The only way you can confront difference and still maintain positive collaborative relationships is through *assertive communication*. Assertive communication involves nonjudgmental descriptions of the differences at hand and suggestions for ways of resolving them. Assertive communication allows you to disclose your feelings about a difference without affixing blame and clarifies the effects of another person's ideas, beliefs, opinions, or positions on you. In other words, assertive communication is a straightforward communication technique designed to confront differences in a nonthreatening, factual, and direct manner for the benefit of both parties.

Assertive communication enables you to maintain self-respect, personal happiness, confidence, and satisfaction with another person. This type of communication allows you to stand up for your ideas, beliefs, opinions, or positions and express your personal needs, values, and concerns in a direct and appropriate way. While meeting your own needs in this way, you do not violate the needs of other people—instead, you simultaneously help others retain a positive self-concept. Quite simply, true assertiveness is a way of behaving that confirms your own individual worth and dignity while at the same time confirming and maintaining the worth and dignity of others.

One of the most difficult things you can do is to ask another person for honest, direct feedback about the situation at hand. It requires courage to check and validate assumptions, but do not wait until the end of the political interaction to ask for such feedback. You should be seeking input and feedback from others on an ongoing basis, always looking for ways to fine-tune your efforts. Doing so also demonstrates that you are willing to listen and adjust your behaviors.

Assertive communication also consists of an element of forthrightness. Forthrightness consists of conveying a confident and forthright message regarding another person's behavior that is nonjudgmental in tone and includes a transparent disclosure of the effects of the other person's behavior on you. Communicating in a forthright manner ensures that you address problems with people with clarity and respect, which enhances others' understanding of the dysfunctional effects of undesirable behavior and leads to smoother and quicker resolution of the problem.

Negotiator

Regardless of type of organization you work in (fairyland, team-oriented, competitive, or pathological, as described in chapter 1), conflict will exist. Conflict is simply the difference in expectations, needs, interests, and desires of two or more individuals or groups. As such, these individuals or groups are not willing to consider another person's or group's expectations, needs, interests, or desires. To further complicate matters, these individuals and groups are firmly locked into a position that they justify as correct and are willing to fight to keep the status quo. As the gap between the respective positions hardens, the more difficult it is to get the respective parties to consider alternatives, solutions, and options. The longer the opposing positions are allowed to exist, the more difficult it is to discover a middle ground between the positions, and from this, a workable agreement. Serving as negotiator in the face of conflict is another "front wheel" role useful in enhancing you credibility and influence as a political navigator.

To avoid impasses and to achieve desired results, Roger Fisher and William L. Ury, in their classic book *Getting to Yes,* described four basic principles:

1. Separate the people from the problem
2. Focus on interest, not problems
3. Generate a variety of possibilities before deciding what to do
4. Insist that the results be based on some objective standard

When you, as a political navigator, separate people from the problem, you are approaching conflict situations objectively. You are also channeling your energies toward resolving the problems rather than spending energy on interpersonal dynamics. When you focus on interests and not problems, you overcome the biggest problem in negotiation, which is that people take a "position" that they are forced to defend. Therefore, many people are unwilling to make adjustments to avoid conflict. By generating a variety of possibilities before deciding what to do, you are providing a range of solutions that people can embrace. This will allow people to consider various solutions to a problem rather than becoming fixated on a specific one. Developing an objective standard equips you with a means of evaluating all possible outcomes, which in turn provides tangible evidence that the problem being addressed has been satisfactorily resolved.

The most common technique used in resolving conflict is for both negotiating parties to give up something as a means of meeting in the middle. This technique, known as a compromise, is guaranteed to make certain neither party is satisfied with the negotiated outcome. Fisher and Ury recommend that both parties identify their *interests* and structure their communications to achieving this end. In this way, positive relationships are maintained and both parties achieve their needs.

To resolve conflict, a political navigator accepts the role of negotiator. As such, you use negotiation skills to come up with alternatives and solutions as well as identify the interests of all parties in a negotiation situation (see chapter 4). Using these skills, you are working proactively to both prevent unnecessary conflict and aggressively resolve the inevitable conflicts that do arise. In short, your negotiating approach involves (a) proactively monitoring other people for sources of conflict, (b) working aggressively to constructively resolve conflict, (c) bringing the parties involved in the conflict together to work through the issue, and (d) ensuring that the proposed resolution is implemented immediately. Following this approach elevates you to the vital role of diplomat.

To be truly effective as a negotiator, you must be comfortable with ambiguity. This means that you are at ease with the unknown and rely on your intuition as a guide when critical facts are unavailable. The more comfortable you can make yourself with ambiguity, the better a leader you will be.

There are number of important factors that contribute to a negotiator's power. These factors include information, organizational authority, appropriate deadlines, legitimacy, and alternatives. Negotiators are more powerful when they have the information they need and are well prepared. They are more powerful when they have a full endorsement of the organization or constituency and have good options to computing a negotiated agreement. Further, they are powerful when they do not need to resolve conflict under some imposed deadline and have the power of an organization's rules, policies, and procedures to back them, and also when they have the freedom to consider options and alternatives. On the other hand, negotiators are less powerful when one or more of the above factors is operating against them and when one or more of the above factors resides on their opponent's side.

Negotiators are powerful when they have strong reputations for being persuasive, tenacious, and possessed of integrity. By persuasive, I mean having the ability to argue a point of view eloquently and convincingly. Persuasiveness is derived from how effective you all are at using the information at hand to build a case for what you want. This includes strong logical reasoning and good communication and interpersonal skills. Tenacity refers to a negotiator's persistence. It helps you discover that there are many possibilities and opportunities behind another person's opposition to your recommendations and suggestions. Finally, integrity refers to your trustworthy, honest, and principled behavior. If your character is questionable, so are your motives. Therefore, it is critical that you maintain the highest possible integrity when negotiating solutions.

Organizational Expert

Organizational knowledge is a prerequisite to becoming politically effective. When such knowledge is demonstrated, you will be viewed as a serious contributor to the organization's strategic initiatives. It will also help you engage in political interactions that improve your organization's effectiveness. Finally, you demonstrate organizational expertise by revealing an understanding of people's needs and expectations. Thus, you adapt your practices, procedures, and political interactions and engagements in order to better serve others. This is clearly a "back wheel" role because it is directly linked to your understanding of your business/organization, professional competency, and technical expertise.

Organizational experts anticipate business trends and processes and break them down into manageable units for others to understand and implement. By dismantling business trends and processes into manageable components, you generate a variety of solutions that narrow the gap between what is needed and what is delivered, making the necessary adjustments to ensure organizational success. As an organizational expert, you demonstrate operational insight and organizational knowledge, which improve your impact and influence. Moreover, you demonstrate an understanding of the philosophy that guides the organization's actions. Acute insight and operational understanding will maximize your knowledge and ability to improve the organization's performance, which in turn helps you generate pertinent, practical solutions for people. Consequently, it is critical for you to understand why people behave the way they do, understand how things get done inside the organization, and how and why decisions are made.

A key area of expertise for organizational experts is the ability to allocate resources in an efficient and effective manner. This requires you to maintain the correct balance between work demands and resources allocation, identifying legitimate demands on people, and helping them focus by setting priorities. Further, you identify creative ways of leveraging resources so people do not feel overwhelmed by what is expected of them.

Organizational experts determine whether other people respond to demanding situations appropriately. This will help you make better people-related decisions and recommendations during a political interaction. As a way of achieving better people-related decisions and recommendations, David Ulrich, in his classic *Human Resource Champions,* writes that effective organizational experts ask the following questions:

1. Does the work environment and culture provide opportunities for celebration, fun, excitement, and openness?
2. Are people compensated and rewarded for work accomplishments?
3. Do people control key decision-making processes that determine how work is done?
4. Do people have a vision and direction that commits them to working hard?
5. Are people given challenging work assignments that provide opportunities to learn new skills?
6. Do people work in teams or collaboratively to accomplish goals?
7. Do people have access to and use of technology that makes their work easier?
8. Do people have the competencies (skills and knowledge) necessary to do their work well?
9. Do people enjoy open, candid, and frequent communications with managers and supervisors?
10. Are people treated with dignity while differences are openly shared and respected?

Finding the answers to these questions enables you to demonstrate your ability to determine the adequacy of involvement, people control, and commitment to the organization. The answers determine the degree to which collaboration and teamwork are employed, the adequacy of organizational culture, and the type of challenging work provided to people. The answers also will and identify the quality and quantity of organizational communications, the quality of the compensation and reward system used, concern for due process, adequacy of technology, and competence.

As an or;anizational expert, you devote most of your time to guaranteeing th at the organization is able to answer to each of the above ten questions positively . By doing so, you are able to enhance your organizational impact and influence.

Demonstrating Business Acumen. Although many managers are experts in one or more technical area useful to the organization, this is of little value to the organization unless you are able to demonstrate understanding of business concepts, methodologies, practices, and operations—in short, business acumen. When business acumen is high, you think like your clients, understand how things get done inside the organization and how and why decisions are made. As such, you have a solid understanding of common practices of finance, marketing, manufacturing, management, organizational behavior, economics, quantitative analysis, decision theory, operations, and business strategy. Knowledge of business fundamentals, systems theory, organizational culture, and politics reveals an understanding of the organizational philosophy that guides business action. Thorough business understanding enables you to adapt your practices and activities to changing business and economic conditions; this understanding also guides you in generating pertinent, practical and politically sensitive solutions for your clients.

One of the first steps in developing business acumen is to learn the language of the organization, which can be accomplished by attending some trade shows associated with the organization's business or products, reading the organization's annual reports, and scheduling short informational interviews with leading business managers to get their take on where the company is headed. Additionally, you can improve your business acumen by visiting the marketing department and obtaining copies of product brochures and sales collateral and reading the organization's press releases.

Another way of demonstrating business acumen is by understanding the needs and expectations of your clients (internal and external). Effective political navigators adapt their practices, procedures, products, innovations, and services based upon this knowledge, which allows them to better service their clients. Business acumen provides you the credibility to promote business initiatives that help the organization improve its competitive readiness, performance capacity, and renewal capabilities. Thus, business acumen allows you to be a member of the organizational "club" responsible for its improvement. This club is the key to being taken seriously in the organization.

Becoming a political navigator enables you to achieve two simultaneous benefits. First, it helps you achieve better business result by implementing ideas and recommendations that help the organization achieve its strategic business goals and objectives. The second benefit, in turn, is that by achieving better business results, you enhance your credibility and influence in the organization. The following activities increase your understanding of the organization and its industry:

- describing the type of business that the organization is operating
- identifying the three top-selling products or services and the three most profitable products or services
- describing the three newest products or services
- analyzing the financial condition of the organization and comparing it with last year's results
- identifying the organization's top three competitors
- identifying the major trends in the organization and its industry
- identifying the organization's strengths, weaknesses, opportunities, and threats
- isolating the firm's core competencies

Partnership Builder

Because of ever-changing conditions, organizations are forced to adjust constantly. Consequently, political navigators adopt a fifth critical role: that of partnership builder. This is another "front wheel" role that requires strong relationship, communication, and negotiation skills (see chapter 4).

Political navigators form partnerships to improve their organization's responsiveness and competitiveness as well as to enhance their credibility and influence within the organization. Such partnerships are not part of a "fix-it" strategy but rather a continual way of managing political interaction and engagements that, in time, can become divisive, nasty, and possibly career limiting. Partnerships are planned approaches to political interactions and engagements and involve goal setting, action planning, monitoring, feedback, and evaluating results. Partnership building is a long-term oriented activity used to improve your influence and credibility in the organization. You create partnerships to help improve the relationships between you and others in the organizations. Partnerships rely on the collaborative involvement of all parties involved in political interactions and engagements. These partnerships provide you opportunities for influencing the manner in which work is accomplished, decisions are made, and roles and responsibilities are allocated.

What is a Partnership? Partners mutually share in the risks and benefits that result from political interactions and engagements. They consist of two or more persons or groups jointly participating in a political interaction or engagement and sharing in both the benefits and risks associated with such ventures. The success of these activities relies solely upon the partners' mutual cooperation and collaboration. Communication is therefore critical to such partnerships—without it, partners may be going in different directions, thus preventing successful achievement of desired objectives.

Securing buy-in from all partnership participants is critical to the partnership's success. If people fail to understand their impact on the partnership, the initiative will not be successful. Partnership success also depends on anticipating problems. The more you know about your partners, the more likely you will be able to anticipate problems and respond proactively. Through partnership exchanges, you will learn a lot about the organization—its people, processes, and practices—which will help you in future decision making. This creates a "knowledge bank" that can be drawn upon to resolve problems and achieve desired results. Taking this concept to the next logical level, you become a coach within a partnership, responsible for information sharing, problem resolution, and providing feedback and reinforcement. This critical, collaborative process is instrumental in your ultimate success as a political navigator.

Partnership involves identifying the needs and expectations of other people. The following are steps to take to guarantee that the partnership is successful:

• Identify all parties involved in the partnership
• Identify and communicate the respective needs and expectations of all participants
• Allow time for all participants to understand the value of the partnership relationship
• Define members' roles and responsibilities within the partnership
• Encourage partners to discuss problems or issues of mutual interest
• Establish focus groups made up of partners to ensure a proactive, collaborative approach to problem solving

Taking these actions will help you create synergistic relationships and promote mutual sharing of information and ideas.

Why are Partnerships Important? Creating partnerships is one of the most important activities in which political navigators can engage. Alliance building allows you to develop mutually beneficial, empathic relationships with your clients, resulting in their satisfaction and achievement of objectives. Partnerships are long term and interdependent, allowing you to better understand and anticipate your clients' needs. These partnerships help you develop the responsive attitude necessary for you to become service oriented.

Creating partnerships helps break down walls between you and your clients in the organization. As a result, lasting commitments are developed and all parties make investments in political interactions and engagements. Thus, you become immersed in the problems, needs, concerns, and expectations of others. This enhances your organizational influence and improves your overall organizational impact. Partnerships allow you to develop a responsive attitude that enables you to develop a client-service orientation. Partnerships enable you to develop trust and honesty with others, allowing for the sharing of ideas, perspectives, and vision for the organization's future.

Partnerships also promote the establishment of working relationships based on shared values, aligned purposes and visions, and mutual support. Partnerships allow people to develop five basic values:

1. Trust—honest exchange devoid of hidden agendas
2. Accountability—personal responsibility for the partnership
3. Support—commitment to giving and receiving support
4. Truth—honest sharing of ideas and feelings
5. Effort—commitment to the mission

Creating partnerships demonstrates your willingness to intimately know those you serve, as well as your ability to learn from clients. Furthermore, partnerships are based upon the needs of clients, not on selfishly advancing your position or creating leverage over others. Consequently, political navigators direct all efforts at satisfying their clients' needs and expectations while making every effort to achieve the desired result and outcomes (see discussion of conflict management styles in chapter 2).

Another compelling reason to create partnerships is to help you establish credibility within the organization. Improved credibility results from your ability to demonstrate professional expertise as well as their understanding of organizational operations and culture. In this way, you are able to provide real value to the organization.

Partnerships help you decide which political interactions and engagements provide the highest value and have the greatest impact on the organization. Armed with such information, you are in a better position to appropriate the resources (time, energy, effort) that will maximize organizational performance and results.

Creating partnerships produces economic utility, which is measured in terms of improved relationships and increased organizational effectiveness and efficiency. Overall, such alliances afford you and your clients opportunities to work in harmony for the purpose of improving the economic viability of the organization, and a healthy organization benefits everyone.

Activities of a Partnership Builder. As partnership builders, political navigators engage in a number of interdependent activities. They examine the organization's efforts to determine their respective values and benefits, allowing decision makers to make critical choices about the actions that most positively impact the organization. Partnership builders create a positive work environment enabling political solutions to be adopted and supported by organizational leaders, managers, and critical employees. They help people make positive developmental decisions that help in improving their long-term career expertise. Partnership builders identify why people participate in some political interactions and engagements and not others, which enables you to understand people's motives and how to adjust accordingly.

RESPONSIBILITIES OF POLITICAL NAVIGATORS

As a political navigator, you accept a variety of new and exciting responsibilities. Each is designed to maximize your effectiveness during political interactions, improve your influence and credibility in the organization, and help you accomplish political engagements that enhance your stature in an organization. The ultimate outcome achieved by way of these responsibilities is improving your organizational effectiveness, and thus, your credibility and career advancement opportunities. The responsibilities include:

- Developing synergistic relationships
- Improving organizational communication
- Demonstrating organizational knowledge
- Identifying and solving problems
- Building consensus and commitment

Developing Synergistic Relationships

One way of achieving your organization's political objectives is for you to improve your relationship skills. This helps you feel good about your interaction and involvement with others. By doing so, you will be perceived as an empathic and caring person who focuses your energies on building relationships and fulfilling the developmental and psychological needs of others. Daniel Goleman, in his classic book *Working with Emotional Intelligence*, writes (1998), "a key social ability is empathy, understanding other's feelings and taking their perspectives, and respecting the differences in how people feel about things. Relationships are a major focus, including learning to be good listeners and questioners; distinguishing between what someone says or does and your own reaction and judgments; being assertive rather that aggressive or passive; and learning the art of cooperation, conflict resolution, and negotiating compromise" (p 268).

Another component of relationship building is synergy, which can be defined as the interaction between individuals whose combined efforts are more influential than if they were to work alone. Synergistic relationships, therefore, are the interdependence of individuals working toward a common goal, which simultaneously provides for growth and development opportunities for both the participants as well as the organization. Synergistic relationships are healthy relationships between you and another person, which yield five benefits:

1. Enhancing and building self-esteem
2. Improving productivity
3. Improving and building organizational communications
4. Enhancing and building organizational understanding
5. Facilitating and building organizational commitment

   To better understand synergistic relationships, complete the following exercise. Take a piece of paper and draw two columns. The header for one column is "characteristics of healthy working relationships" and the other "characteristics of unhealthy working relationships." List what you perceive to be indicative of both a healthy and an unhealthy relationship. Most of what exists in an unhealthy relationship can be found in the workplace while those elements of healthy relationships can be found in your personal life.
   Let me ask you two additional questions:

1. What elements produce healthy personal relationships?
2. Why can't they be at the center of all political interactions and engagements?

Typically, freedom to participate is an important ingredient in personal relationships. In other words, you have a choice but is this always the case? What about your family? Most healthy relationships, including those with your family members and personal friends, are the result of free will. However, professionally (in organizations), people are "stuck" working with certain types of people that make it difficult to produce positive synergy. Sometimes working relationships are better than personal ones, but not typically. To promote positive, healthy working relationships, you must understand how to establish, cultivate, and improve them. In other words, develop an approach that can be used to build positive, healthy, and synergistic relationships.
   An eight-step process for building positive, healthy, and synergistic relationships is as follows: freedom from fear, communication, interaction, acceptance, personal involvement, trust, honesty, and self-esteeming (Figure 3.2).

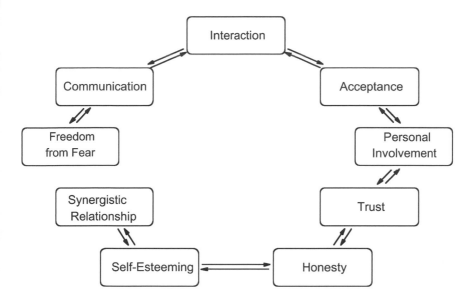

Figure 3.2. Synergistic Relationship Model

Freedom from Fear. Work environments where fear is common are characterized by reprisals and intimidation and will cause frustration, anger, and resentment. Interpersonal relationships cannot survive under these conditions. However, a fearless relationship allows you and others to communicate, take risks, and work collectively together. In a fear-free environment, creativity flourishes and people are challenged and stimulated to solve complex problems, which allows both sides the opportunity to build a positive relationship that ultimately benefits the organization.

Communication. Even in organizations free of fear, communication can deteriorate. Ineffective managers allow only one-way communication, from themselves to others in the organization. Some are willing to communicate but have poor listening skills, which discourages communications.

Many times messages are misunderstood because people possess different frames of reference, experiences, language, or use different terms. To overcome this, you encourage two-way communication, making certain to interact on the same level and using the same language as another person.

Interaction. To have positive and healthy, fear-free, mistake-free communication, personal interaction must be fostered. Political navigators are not afraid of face-to-face contact with other people. For example, e-mail is convenient and efficient; it can also present a barrier to interpersonal interaction, while person-to-person political interactions are vital to developing rapport. Political navigators understand such slight distinctions and avoid using the wrong medium for communications, which promotes improved interactions.

Acceptance. Synergistic relationships are nonjudgmental but accepting. Therefore, acceptance means being ready to listen to and consider what other people have to say. If you dismiss other people's input, the relationship becomes one-way, very weak, and nonsupportive.

Personal Involvement. Political navigators know that the people they interact with are human beings and they treat them accordingly. This does not mean that every personal detail of one's life is shared with others, but it does mean showing concern and interest in others as persons of worth. This approach goes a long way in cultivating trust.

Trust. Trust can only be established if the relationship between you and another person exemplifies truth, confidence, mutual respect, and reliability. Trust assures all parties that all necessary, vital information will be shared, proposed solutions will be free of bias, and confidentiality will be respected. Thus, there are no hidden agendas. Other people will refuse to build long-term relationships with you if you are perceived as being untrustworthy.

Honesty. Synergistic relationships depend on total honesty in word, deed, and intention. At all times, you must adhere to the truth—even if that means presenting others with information they would rather avoid. Honesty is in the best interest of all parties.

Self-esteeming. When all the other components of a healthy relationship—freedom from fear, communication, interaction, acceptance, personal involvement, trust, and honesty—have been achieved, the result will be higher self-esteem for all parties. At this point, the relationship becomes synergistic—the whole is greater than the sum of its parts (see chapter 1). The more you respect yourself and others, the more other people will respect themselves and you. Quite simply, reciprocity in the relationship can only enhance the self-esteem of both parties. At this point, you are operating as a political navigator in an organization.

Improving Organizational Communication

As a political navigator, you are responsible for interpreting and sharing information and for motivating people to engage in political engagements and implement change. Communications is essential in this process. However, too many organizations view communications as a one-time, splashy announcement that publicizes the initiation of a political engagement (see chapter 6). Afterwards, there is dead silence for the duration of the engagement. This one-time communication approach can create initial excitement and enthusiasm but is quickly replaced with cynicism and criticism. A better strategy is to use both formal and informal communication as a way of mobilizing people into action. As such, it is essential that you use a two-way, interactive communication approach, which is always more powerful than one-way communication. Otherwise, you cannot be assured of staying in touch with your people, nor can you be assured that communications are being received as sent. Therefore, there is questioning: What's going on? Why? How does this fit together?

Political navigators use every means possible to communicate their ideal vision, ideas, suggestions, and recommendations. Accordingly, they create a communications plan to achieve their goals. An effective communications plan is a simple document free of jargon and technical language. It illuminates a verbal picture incorporating all possible media and forums (i.e., memos, e-mail, and newsletters, plus formal and informal interactions). Such plans utilize repetition. This allows ideas to be understood and fully comprehended. Finally, an effective communications plan relies on leadership by example in that the behavior of political navigators is consistent with the message being communicated.

A communications strategy is the foundation of every political interaction and engagement. It is very important that you communicate effectively with all persons affected by a political engagement (see chapter 6).

However, it is not the intent of this book to teach you how to build a detailed communications strategy. A number of outstanding resources are available on this subject (see chapter 8) and you are strongly advised to read as much as you can on the subject. At a minimum, you address the following:

- Audiences: What are the major categories of people with whom you will communicate and what are their information needs?
- Messages: How will you articulate your messages to identify with the particular frames of reference related to the audiences you just identified?
- Media: For each audience, what is its preferred means of receiving information (e.g., e-mail, paper memos, informal meetings with the boss, presentations)?
- Frequency: Depending upon each audience group and the impact they will feel (both perceived and real), what is an appropriate timeline for each audience that will provide them with a rate and flow of information that keeps them moving smoothly through the political interaction?

Sharing Information. When people have access to accurate and timely information, they feel they are part of political interactions and engagements. Ultimately, your goal is to build strong relationships, starting early in a political interaction and/or engagement and maintaining those relationships in ways that are meaningful and useful to each person you interact with.

Inclusion can be realized by simply providing courtesy copies of updates and reports to interested parties. The content will vary, naturally, by the needs of each individual and by the sensitivity of the information. But as pointed out earlier (see discussion of sources of power in chapter 2), those with informal power (expert) can many times be your most threatening barriers. These individuals' only need is the basic and ongoing information about a situation that affects them. Your difficulties, however, may arise with those with more formal power (legitimate) who are afraid of sharing too much information, too soon, or at all. Unfortunately, we still have organizational leaders who see the withholding of information as power. By giving up information to "others in the organization," they perceive themselves as losing that power of knowledge and information that only a select few were privy to before.

As a political navigator, you discuss with these organizational leaders the value of open, honest, and ongoing communications and how such information can move political interactions and engagements forward. Involve them in, or at least share with them, the process of getting others participating in decision making and action planning. In doing so, organizational leaders will discover that most people's basic need is no more complex than information sharing.

When you share information, you are fulfilling the traditional role of a political navigator. As such, your primary responsibility is to the provide information needed by others in order for them to define problems and make decisions. As such, you are responsible for supplying information, helping people cope with political engagements, and handling defensive reactions.

Demonstrating Organizational Knowledge

Credible political navigators understand that they are responsible for demonstrating an understanding of their organization. Typically, this includes an understanding of how your organization operates, how decisions are made, who has influence in the organization, who interacts with whom, and how business gets done. Failure to actively demonstrate your organizational knowledge will reduce your credibility, which will limit your effectiveness in implementing political interactions and engagements.

Most organizations are complex, hierarchical structures comprised of divisions and departments organized to produce products and services. This cold, impersonal, linear arrangement is how most organizations are depicted. Unfortunately, we often forget that organizations are made up of people. In fact, people constitute all aspects of organizational life. They do not randomly reside within organizations. Each person has his or her selected purpose for existence and assigned responsibilities for tasks and activities that produce outputs necessary for the survival of the organization. As we discussed in chapter 1, it is occasionally useful to think of organizations from both formal and informal vantage points. Building on this concept, it helpful to think of organizations as icebergs where you only see the part above the surface (formal). This represents the official components of the image the organization wishes to project, or what executives want you to think the firm represents. Beneath the water's surface lies the informal, real organization: the hierarchical layers, departments, units, functions, policies, procedures, practices, managerial relationships, and so forth.

Another way of thinking about an organization's system is by examining the dynamic interdependence of its essential elements. Figure 3.3 provides an overview. The arrows in both directions convey an open system principle, illustrating how each of seven elements of an organization is connected to—and has effects upon—other elements. If an organization is healthy and producing positive results, these seven interdependent elements are working in harmony. When an organization fails to achieve desired results, you can look to the relationships among these elements to reveal potential breakdowns and/or areas of weakness. Once a breakdown has been discovered, it is useful to examine these elements in greater

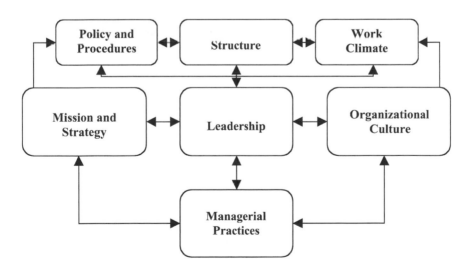

Figure 3.3. Organizational Systems Model

detail. While it is essential to examine each element on its own carefully, it proves more important to assess the elements' interdependence and relationships to discover the potential for embracing political interactions and engagements. Consequently, organizational initiatives can be targeted to improve various elements of organizational system. Thus, you will have a systematic approach to examining weaknesses as well as looking for opportunities for improvement between and among these seven elements.

The heart of every organization is its leaders. Therefore, the center of an organizational system is leadership. The leadership's skills and abilities impact and influence the organization's direction while energizing, exciting, and influencing its workforce. Moreover, leadership directly influence the four most important functions within the organization—those of mission and strategy, organizational culture, structure, and managerial practice Indirectly, leadership influences policies and procedures and work climate, which are mostly impacted by such things as organizational structure, mission and strategy, policies and procedures, managerial practices, organizational culture, and work climate. The distance between various functions is also significant. For example, change in organizational structure may not directly affect its culture unless leadership and work climate change simultaneously. Moreover, structural change may or may not have an impact on the organization's mission and strategy unless leadership deems it necessary and policies and procedures are altered significantly. Similarly, improvements in managerial practices may not significantly affect an organization's policies and procedures unless the structure, leadership, and mission and strategy are altered to reflect these improvements. Change in policies and procedures may not impact work climate or culture unless structural considerations, managerial practices, and leadership are fully supportive of these changes. Even though leadership blesses policy or procedural changes, in reality many changes occurring deep inside individual departments are rarely, if ever, fully disclosed to senior management. Consequently, departments may vary so drastically in their interpretations of organizational rules and regulations that, over time, a somewhat schizophrenic work climate and culture is the result. Improving the interaction between and among these elements will affect your ability to bring about organizational change within the organization, which ultimately affects your credibility, and thus, your influence.

Identifying and Solving Problems

Unfortunately, many organizations cannot correctly solve or even identify their own problems, which provides you with a real opportunity to enhance your political influence in the organization. To become a political navigator, you accept the responsibility for being a problem solver in your organization. Identifying and dealing with problems can actually help you improve your trustworthiness. Of course, the type and complexity of problems vary from organization to organization and within an organization.

When solving problems, your primary responsibility is making certain that the perceived problem is indeed the one that needs solving. To be effective, therefore, you spend the majority of your time ascertaining the accuracy of the problem rather than providing solutions to problems that do not exist. A helpful method involves working with the problem as "defined" by others in such a way that more useful definitions emerge. Next, simply listen to others and reflect upon their perspective of a situation to gather new insight. Encouraging others to get involved in the problem solving frequently results in improved creativity and innovation. Once people have been encouraged to come forth and participate in problem solving, those who were previously silent can frequently achieve surprising results. In fact, it is possible that you may be the first person that actually encourages others to voice their ideas or resistance. Certainly you will see a greater involvement in problem solving, ownership, and commitment to solutions once you have successfully involved others.

Once you understand the problem from various vantage points, identify alternative approaches to resolving the problem. Many times this helps you reap better results than adopting a singular plan of action. Remember, people are encouraged to define existing problems and test alternatives for an effective resolution. To execute this responsibility correctly, you can use a partnership approach in which you focus your attention on identifying problems and selecting, evaluating, and implementing alternatives. Next, identify your people's readiness and commitment to a political engagement. The following questions can be used to achieve this end:

- How willing is the organization to implement a political solution identified during the political engagement process?
- Are senior managers willing to adopt a political solution?
- What types of information does the organization readily accept or resist?
- What are people's attitudes toward the political solution?
- What are senior managers' attitudes toward the political solution?
- To what extent will people regard their contribution to resolving the conflict as a legitimate and desirable objective?

Another way of gauging readiness for the political solution is to examine the level of enthusiasm for a particular recommendation. By identifying the level of enthusiasm, you instantaneously measure resistance to or support for a given solution. Once identified, you are able to withdraw or encourage recommendations prior to implementation. Remember to present alternative solutions instead of a single solution. Offer analysis of the pros and cons for each alternative. By discussing these alternatives, you are engaging the other people in a greater degree of "ownership" of the final solution or approach. They will inherently assume a shared responsibility for the ultimate success or failure of the solution.

Becoming a political navigator requires you to take an active role in the problem-solving process. Your objectivity helps you evaluate existing problems and explain possible solutions. In addition, you use a synergistic approach, collaborating with people in the perceptual, cognitive, and action-taking processes involved in solving organizational problems. In the final analysis, every time you address a problem, you have an opportunity to further clarify the personal interests, values, and expectations of other people, which enhances your influence in the organization as well.

Building Consensus and Commitment

Any political solution useful to an organization will rely on people working together. As a political navigator, you build consensus and commitment among organizational decision makers for bringing about lasting and needed change. Each person in the organization is encouraged to consider the overall good of the organization before considering personal objectives or goals. Therefore, you provide sound and convincing recommendations and present them persuasively.

Building consensus and commitment requires you to use a collaborative, participatory approach with people during problem identification and resolution. This requires you to establish a synergistic relationship with other people. In fact, synergistic relationships are a collaborative search for acceptable answers to people's real needs and concerns. Ideally, this will be a mutually beneficial relationship in which trust and a readiness for change are developed quickly during the political interaction and engagement processes.

Establishing a Sense of Urgency. A particular strategy for building consensus and commitment is to establish a sense of urgency for a political solution. This is important to gain needed cooperation. When complacency is high among people, they are not willing to embrace change. Consequently, the political solution usually goes nowhere. Without a sense of urgency, it is nearly impossible to energize people to address problems within the organization. Thus, the momentum for a political solution never materializes.

People find a thousand ingenious ways to withhold support from important political solutions that they sincerely think are unnecessary. Some organizations maintain a heightened capacity for denial while others promote a kill-the-messenger culture that adds to complacency. Still others have overconfident executives and senior managers who resist political interactions and engagements. Any of these excuses can lead to apathy and indifference.

There are several positive ways to raise the urgency level within people. As such, you make available more data about the levels of satisfaction that people experienced by adopting similar suggestions and recommendations. You provide more relevant data and honest discussion during conversations with others and promote honest discussions of problems and insist that senior managers stop providing "happy talk" about real, serious political issues. Finally, you provide people with information on future opportunities, or increased financial incentives for capitalizing on opportunities that result from political interactions and engagements.

CONCLUSION

Working with people is the hardest thing you will ever do. To become a political navigator, you adopt the roles of a relationship builder, assertive communicator, negotiator, organizational expert, and partnership builder to work effectively with others. Further, you must accept your responsibilities for developing synergistic relationships, improving organizational communication, demonstrating organizational knowledge, identifying and solving problems, and building consensus and commitment in the organization. When these roles and responsibilities have been successfully executed, you are well on your way to becoming a political navigator— one who has credibility and influence in an organization and is capable of successfully executing any political interaction or engagement.

REFERENCES

Fisher, Roger, and William L. Ury. *Getting to Yes: Negotiating Agreements without Giving In.* New York and New Rutherford, NJ: Penguin, 1991.
Goleman, Daniel. *Working with Emotional Intelligence.* New York: Bantam Books, 1998.
Rogers, Carl R. *On Becoming a Person.* Boston: Houghton Mifflin, 1961.
Ulrich, David. *Human Resource Champions.* Cambridge, MA: Harvard Business School Press, 1997.

FOUR

Political Navigators' Skills

This chapter examines several skills useful to the ultimate success of a political navigator. These skills are used during political interactions and engagements. There are also useful when resolving conflicts, negotiating, and building relationships and partnerships. This chapter will explore relationship, communication, conflict resolution, partnership, organizational understanding, and political thinking skills.

RELATIONSHIP SKILLS

Relationship skills allow political navigators to enhance their relationships with other people in the organization. They help you build a positive, comfortable, and nonthreatening communication climate with others—one that encourages people to discuss organizational issues, problems, and other ideas openly and honestly, without fear of reprisal. Such an environment establishes conditions that will expedite the synergistic relationship process (see chapter 3). Accordingly, the first rule in relationship building with another person is for you to listen, truly hearing what another person is saying, both verbally and nonverbally. This requires listening, observing, and empathizing skills to enable you to really hear what others are saying and to pick up on what is "between the lines" of a message.

Improving relationships requires you to shift your managerial style from authoritarian to participatory. This is done by relinquishing control and dominance over other people and allowing them to participate as equal partners. Thus, recognize and accept that others have a great deal of experience, insight, and expertise that needs to be acknowledged, tapped, and applied. In order to demonstrate the value and importance of others' ideas and thoughts, you become an active participant during political interactions.

Once a participatory managerial style has been established, continue using your interpersonal skills to gather important information from others. Encourage them to share their feelings and provide moments of silence that can help others reflect and reconsider their ideas, thoughts, and positions. These skills serve as road map helping you maneuver and adjust to the ebbs and flows of communication during exchanges with others.

The ultimate outcome of a positive relationship with another person is known as rapport, which is the unconditional positive regard between you and another person. Rapport is more than a superficial relationship; it is a deep concern for the well-being of others. It can be demonstrated when you are as interested in others as you are in the results they produce. Rapport is established through your sincere interest in and acceptance of others.

Rapport is further enhanced when you are emotionally empathetic. This is demonstrated when you are empathically attuned to the emotions and feelings of others. However, successful political navigators understand that most political interactions and engagements are messy, and at times, decidedly emotional, especially for politically unconscious incompetent individuals, who often do not have the same adaptability you do. The emotions of such individuals are normal and inevitable, and therefore cannot be ignored. Practicing emotional empathy raises holistic understanding and engages others, thereby gaining more interpersonal leverage.

Interpersonal Relationship Styles

Clearly, differences between people are not the only sources of interpersonal tension and conflict. Differences are, however, a major factor in misunderstanding and resistance. Since other people are important to your success, it is important to discover why they think, make decisions, and use time differently than you. Additionally, other people may communicate, handle emotions, manage stress, and deal with conflicting opinions differently, which is not necessarily a bad thing, although these differences can lead to negative political interactions.

In the 1960s, Dr. David Merrill identified two clusters of behavior: *assertiveness* and *responsiveness*. These two dominions are incredibly helpful in predicting how other people are likely to behave. These key dimensions of behavior combine to form the interpersonal relationship styles model (Figure 4.1).

Assertiveness. In this model, *assertiveness is the degree to which a person is perceived as attempting to influence the thoughts and actions of others.* It is helpful to think of a continuum of assertiveness, in which a person's behavior is typically more assertive or less assertive than that of half the population.

Responsiveness. Responsiveness is the other crucial dimension of behavior in this model. *Responsiveness is the degree to which a person is perceived as expressing feelings when relating with others.* It is helpful to think of a continuum of responsiveness in which a person's behavior is typically more responsive or less responsive than that of half the population.

Four Interpersonal Styles. Each individual's interpersonal style is his or her own unique blend of two dimensions: assertiveness and responsive-

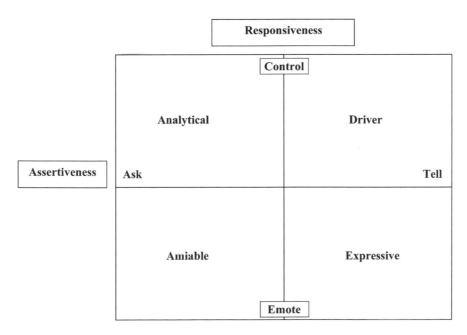

Figure 4.1. Interpersonal Relationship Styles Model
Source: Adapted from Merrill and Reid, 1981.

ness. Nevertheless, most people fall more or less into one or another of the four styles known as *analytical, driver, amiable,* or *expressive.* These four styles can be described this way:

- *Analytical style* is perceived as *control-responsive/ask-assertive.* Analyticals are task oriented, precise, and thorough. Analyticals like to deal in facts, work methodically, and use standard operating procedures. They are motivated by a need for *respect* and their specialty is *technical.*
- *Driver style* is perceived as *control-responsive/tell-assertive.* Drivers are goal-oriented, disciplined, determined "bottom-line" thinkers who push for results and accomplishments. Their motivation is *power* and their specialty is *control.*
- *Amiable style* is perceived as *emote-responsive/ask-assertive.* Amiables are people oriented, friendly, accepting, cooperative, and like to be liked. Amiables are motivated to help others in a team effort. The payoff for them is *approval* and their specialty is *supportive.*
- *Expressive style* is perceived as *emote-responsive/tell-assertive.* Expressives are idea oriented, vigorous, enthusiastic, and spontaneous. Expressives thrive on *recognition.* Their specialty is *social* and they like to initiate relationships and motivate others toward goals.

Developing versatility begins when you identify what people want and understand what drives or motivates each individual interpersonal style. The following is a guide to relating most effectively to each interpersonal style to improve your versatility.

Improving Interpersonal Relationships with Analyticals. Analyticals value hard work and attention to detail and situations for them must be logical and carefully worked out. When working with analyticals, you can enhance your versatility by:

- sticking to business;
- using action words rather than feeling words;
- providing solid, realistic evidence and support for decision making;
- preparing your "case" in advance;
- approaching them in a straightforward way;
- supporting their principles when possible;
- presenting materials in an organized manner, making certain that you clearly communicate important ideas and facts;
- using a step-by-step timetable, assuring them there won't be surprises when preparing a schedule for implementing action;
- avoiding casual, loud, or informal conversations;

- being precise and organized and not using opinion words (others' or your own) as evidence;
- avoiding guesses and being accurate whenever possible;
- not being disorganized or rushing the decision-making process;
- avoiding leaving things to chance or luck;
- avoiding aggressive behavior, being unrealistic with deadlines, or being vague about what is expected of them and always following through.

Improving Interpersonal Relationships with Drivers. Drivers need information that allows them to make decisions quickly and get tangible results. They also like to know they are in charge. When working with drivers, you can enhance your versatility by:

- being clear, specific, brief, and to the point;
- always dealing with the facts, packaging them for quick decision making;
- using results that support their conclusions and actions;
- sticking to business;
- coming prepared with all requirements, objectives, and support material in a well-organized presentation;
- always presenting the facts logically and planning your presentation efficiently;
- asking specific questions and providing them alternatives and choices for making their own decisions;
- departing graciously after concluding your business;
- avoiding trying to build personal relations and not wasting their time;
- not being inefficient, disorganized, messy, or rambling on;
- avoiding conversations that distract them from the business at hand;
- not asking rhetorical questions;
- not going to a meeting with a ready-made decision;
- never trying to convince them to support an idea through "personal" appeals.

Improving Interpersonal Relationships with Amiables. Amiables want warmth, understanding, friendship, and trust in their communications. Their strength is building personal relationships. When working with amiables, you can enhance your versatility by:

- holding open meetings with a personal comment to break the ice and being casual and nonthreatening;

- providing assurances and guarantees, especially for decision making;
- supporting their relationships and feelings and showing sincere interest in them;
- being candid and open;
- listening carefully to what is being said and being responsive;
- presenting your case softly, in a nonthreatening manner;
- watching carefully for possible areas of early disagreement or dissatisfaction;
- moving casually, informally;
- defining clearly (preferably in writing) individual contributions and assuring them that their actions will diminish risks and benefit them;
- not rushing into the business agenda or forcing them to respond quickly;
- avoiding disagreeable subjects and not sticking coldly or harshly to business;
- avoiding debating facts and figures;
- not being vague (rather, offer them options and probabilities);
- not patronizing or demeaning them by using subtlety;
- not being abrupt or rude.

Improving Interpersonal Relationships with Expressives. Expressives need to know you are with them in spirit and they appreciate information that allows them to move, create, or take action. When working with expressives, you can enhance your versatility by:

- asking for their opinions and ideas and supporting their dreams and intentions;
- always talking about people and their goals;
- giving testimony and incentives for decisions;
- leaving time for relating and socializing;
- asking for their opinions/ideas regarding people;
- allowing plenty of time to be stimulating, fun loving, and active;
- providing testimonials from people they see as important and prominent;
- offering special, immediate, and extra incentives for their willingness to take risks;
- avoiding dealing with too many details or being dogmatic, cold, or tight-lipped;
- never talking down to them, legislating over them, or presenting them with too many facts and figures;
- avoiding being boring;
- not leaving decisions hanging in the air;
- not being too task-oriented or judgmental.

COMMUNICATION SKILLS

Communication skills are used to help you improve your exchanges with the people directly and indirectly involved in a political interaction or engagement. Using communication skills helps establish rapport with other people, which leads to more successful political interactions and engagements. These skills can play a critical role in relating successfully with others. Communication skills can be clustered into two categories: following skills and understanding skills

Following Skills

Political navigators use skills that help them understand the thoughts and ideas of others. In order to accomplish this, as a political navigator, you allow others to do most of the talking. There are four skills that help you follow others better during one-on-one conversations. They are: *active listening, questioning, encouraging,* and *silence.*

Active Listening. Good listening is the foundation of the empathetic behavior previously discussed and is an important bridge to understanding others. Accordingly, a key to effective communications is to become a better listener. In fact, approximately 70 percent of a manager's day is spent in communication and over half of that time involves listening. Feedback is a critical element in effective communication and can be made accurate through good listening.

The difference between inactive and active listening is the difference between just hearing and listening. The act of listening requires energy, effort, and concentration. Listening readily captures content and intended meaning that others are attempting to convey. Further, active listening conveys respect. When people are listened to attentively, they will believe that their point of view is taken more seriously. They will also state their feelings and thinking more clearly. They will provide feedback that demonstrates respect and listen to others more carefully when they speak. Additionally, they will become less quarrelsome and more receptive to different points of view.

In order to develop better listening skills, concentrate all your physical and mental energies on listening, demonstrate interest and alertness, and seek an area of agreement with others. When possible, search for meaning and avoid getting hung up on specific words, avoid interrupting the speaker, and demonstrate patience (people can "listen faster" than others can speak). Provide clear and unambiguous feedback to others, repress the tendency to respond emotionally to what is said, and ask questions when you do not understand something. Finally, withhold evaluation of the message until the other person is finished and you are sure you understand the message.

Questioning. Questions are used to direct the conversation into more constructive and informative channels. Questions may be directed at an entire group or a specific person. Questioning is a powerful tool with which to guide the flow and direction of conversation, facilitate group discussion, and help you obtain specific information. Basically, two types of questions are useful: closed- and open-ended.

Closed-ended questions have specific responses and can be answered in relatively few words. They are important for guiding the conversation and gathering essential information quickly. Examples of a closed-ended question might be, *"How long have you been in your current position?"* or *"Is this a problem you would like to solve?"* This type of question is concerned with gathering needed information rather than with the effectiveness of the response or the feelings of others.

In contrast, *open-ended questions* generally encourage another person to expand the conversation in several different directions and require more than a few words to answer. They also help people to prepare to consider divergent points of view or widen their perceptual field. Open-ended questions open the doors to developing a good rapport and positive relationship. An open-ended question allows people to convey their point of view and is less threatening to others. An example might be, *"How do you feel about the effectiveness of the new marketing program?"* People answering this type of question may take several different approaches.

Encouraging. Encouraging enables people to continue to elaborate on their thoughts and feeling. Supportive remarks by you such as *"I understand,"* *"It's OK to feel that way,"* *"That's interesting, tell me more,"* or *"I hear you"* are useful in countering feelings of inadequacy. They also prompt action by encouraging people to continue the discussion. Another effective skill is an "umm-hum" or a nod of the head to let others know you are listening. This serves to strengthen a person's response and his or her efforts to continue speaking.

Silence. The use of silence is a somewhat difficult skill to master but enables the person speaking to provide additional information or explanation, if appropriate or needed, and think through what has transpired. However, even experienced political navigators are initially uncomfortable with silence as a technique. However, with practice, it becomes obvious that intentional silence provides people the opportunity to explore their feelings more deeply and provide them with additional time to think about what they are going to say. Additionally, it may provide the less articulate people with a feeling of worth. Sometimes, silence can be overdone; more than a minute of silence, for example, often causes discomfort. Therefore, avoid extensive periods of silence as they may be misinterpreted and perceived as unresponsiveness. Silence is most beneficial when used in combination with other skills, such as active listening and encouraging.

Understanding Skills

Political navigators use skills that help them interpret the thoughts and ideas of others. To accomplish this, use skills that allow others to elaborate, expand, and provide clarity regarding their thoughts and ideas. Six skills help you better understand others during the one-on-one conversations common during political interactions. They are: *interpreting, clarifying, reflecting, summarizing, paraphrasing,* and *tentative analysis.*

Interpreting. Interpreting is used to explain cause-and-effect relationships and clarify implications. This approach generally results in a greater awareness of what is involved and enables people to understand the full ramifications of what another person is saying. Interpreting requires you to draw a conclusion about another person's perception of a situation or event and provides a basis for publicly testing any assumptions made during a conversation. Thus, it allows you the opportunity to verify your own point of view and acknowledge the correctness of your interpretation. Common statements such as *"What I hear you saying ... "* and *"Based upon what you have said..."* can be used to introduce your interpretations.

Clarifying. When political navigators ask another person to elaborate on a particular point or statement or provide an example or illustration to make the meaning more clearly understood, they are using the clarifying technique. Additionally, sometimes it is helpful to make clarifying statements in an attempt to place another person's feeling and attitudes in a clear, more recognizable form and thereby identify the cause of his or her problem. Do not use clarifying to interpret another person's feelings but, rather, to "test" understanding. Using this skill involves asking questions such as *"Are you angry at not being selected to participate in the restructuring project?"*

Reflecting. Reflecting allows you to bring to the surface the substantive content and emotions of another person's words. It is used to illustrate that you understand correctly what others are in experiencing, thinking, or feeling. Reflecting helps you bring out into the open feelings and hidden agendas and to guide the conversation. This is critical because deeply repressed feelings can affect virtually every thought or behavior of other people. Such feelings often negatively affect the political interaction process. Therefore, they need to be brought to the surface to be dealt with effectively, which helps develop open and honest communication. An example of a summarizing statement would be, *"So you are looking for a training program to help you develop interpersonal skills to improve your effectiveness as a supervisor?"*

Summarizing. Summarizing communicates to others the essence of what has been said throughout a political interaction. To make certain that both sides are understood, you may wish to ask another person to agree or disagree with your summary. An example of a summarizing statement is, *"Let me take a moment to summarize our conversation...."* This technique is used to summarize several concepts, ideas, and thoughts and help you to identify the most important of them. Alternatively, you may wish to have another person summarize the discussion as a way of checking for accuracy and understanding. Summarizing differs from paraphrasing in that it is used at the end of a discussion with another person.

Paraphrasing. The primary purpose of paraphrasing is to restate, in your own words, another person's basic message. Paraphrasing is used primarily to test your understanding of what has been said. It is used to communicate to another person that you are trying to understand the basic message and, if successful, that you have been following what a person has said. An example of paraphrasing would be: *"You seem to be saying that his overbearing personality makes it difficult to accomplish the project."*

Tentative Analysis. A tentative analysis is usually stated in the form of a question because it is a "hunch" type of interpretation that is usually narrow in scope. Thus, it is a form of short summarization. Because it generally deals with one thought or concept instead of several, it stops short of being comprehensive. Its principal advantage is that it communicates that you are attempting to test publicly your understanding of another person's message. Doing this one step at a time, you demonstrate respect for another person's viewpoint and patience with them. An example of tentative analysis would be, *"I have a feeling you are not very satisfied with the quality of the sales training program."*

Following and understanding skills enable you to develop a comfortable working relationship with other people—one conducive to sharing ideas and feelings. Such a relationship is essential to the development of rapport with other people.

Questions Helpful in Improving Your Own Communication Effectiveness

Political navigators have control over only themselves during communications with other people. To improve your communications effectiveness, use the following questions as a guide when preparing for a political interaction:

- To what degree does my personal history affect this conversation?
- To what degree is my self-concept at risk?
- How threatened do I feel?

- Did I hear the other person correctly?
- Do I really understand what the other person is saying?
- Given my knowledge of the other person, to what degree might that person be distorting the interaction? In what probable direction?
- How threatened might the other person be at this moment?
- How might I reduce defensiveness?
- Have I made any unjustified assumptions about this interaction or its meaning?
- Does my attitude toward the other person distort my perceptions?
- What is the other person's interpersonal style? How does it match with my own?
- What adjustments might I have to make in order to accommodate this person's interpersonal style?

When you have addressed these question, take appropriate action. This should help improve the quality of your communications.

CONFLICT RESOLUTION SKILLS

During political interactions and engagements, it is difficult to maintain positive interpersonal relationships because people have different agendas, values, beliefs, and interpersonal communication styles. This can take a great toll on all parties personally and produce significant amounts of stress. Therefore, conflict resolution skills are absolutely critical to your success as a political navigator.

Understanding and Dealing with Political Resistance

When political conflict occurs, people resist alternatives, solutions, and options used to resolve the conflict. However, many managers are shocked when it occurs and wish that it would never happen or would just go away. The only solution for dealing with political resistance is to understand its underlying reasons and learn how to address them.

As a political navigator, you understand that political resistance is a very positive opportunity. It allows you to confirm support for your political solutions, as well as to address peoples' fears and vulnerabilities.

In Peter Block's classic book, *Flawless Consulting* (1999), he suggests an interesting question when dealing with resistance: "What are people resisting when they resist you?" Typically, political resistances can be traced to people's differences in dealing with an unpleasant or difficult situation. For example, a person with strong political ties must be transferred to another position. This is not an easy situation to deal with and addressing it may produce defensive behaviors. Why? Resistance is simply the fear of losing one's current state. In fact, resistance is predictable, natural, and a necessary part of learning about another person or implementing a political solution. It is a natural response for people to become defensive. They push back when they feel they are being pushed. One solution might be to present only those alternatives that do not cause them to become defensive, but is this realistic? By addressing political resistance and taking advantage of the opportunities it offers, you improve your credibility and influence and enhance your status in the organization.

When you propose new ideas and innovations or make suggestions and recommendations that resolve political conflict, many people feel uncomfortable. Some people are very vocal and express their displeasure openly, while others express their discomfort indirectly. They remain completely silent and say things like the solution is impractical, we have done that before, or we need more information before we can proceed. Also they tell you that your approach is wrong, they are confused, or the timing is off. Sometimes other people deflect personal responsibility by saying it's not my fault, it's theirs. Additionally, they sabotage the solution by not directly confronting their real concerns. They do not openly express their real difficulties or inadequacies.

Regardless of how people express resistance, it is important to identify the many reasons for political resistance. Here are the most common reasons:

- The purpose of a political solution is not made clear.
- Employees affected by a political solution are not involved in the planning.
- An appeal for a political solution is based on personal reasons.
- There is a fear of failure.
- The cost (personal or organizational) is too high or the rewards inadequate.
- These is a perceived lose of control.
- The vested interest of the individual or subunit of the organization is involved.
- There is a lack of respect and trust in the initiator.
- There is satisfaction with the status quo.
- Past experience with political conflict is negative.
- There is an honest difference of opinion.
- There is a lack of management support for a political solution.

Conflict over resources, conflict over recognition and rewards, lack of commitment to a political solution, lack of an agreed-upon solution, differing organizational values, lack of trust and credibility, and differing realities are other circumstances that can produce resistance.

Political Resistance Resolution Method

During a political conflict, the root cause of resistance is fear. People fear losing control, power, status, authority, or position. People also fear becoming vulnerable. However, most people are too proud to admit it. They often rationalize their behavior or blame others for creating the situation. In the face of change, they resist positive political solutions because they fear the outcomes.

When political resistance occurs, you should not take it personally and become defensive. Political resistance is simply the result of differing perspectives and the fear of losing the status quo. Political navigators who maintain an objective viewpoint will be better able to deal with people's resistance to their ideas, alternatives, and suggestions. You can minimize resistance by presenting political solutions in a timely and orderly fashion. Additionally, you will compromise your integrity by endorsing solutions that, however, popular, do not adequately solve the organization's problems.

Political navigators can address these differing perspectives by using the *political resistance resolution method.* This method can be thought of as a set of skills to govern conflict. It is a constructive process for handling emotion-laden disagreements between you and other people. Its purpose is to bring to the surface underlying fears that cause resistance, so others can understand and accept the proposed solution, change, or alternative being proposed. This method encourages assertive communications and the sharing of feelings but does not permit the typical free-for-all that blocks creative resolution. Quite simply, it is an effective tool for addressing differing perspectives of people. The method consists of four steps: (1) acknowledging political resistance, (2) clarifying political resistance, (3) problem solving, and (4) confirming the answer.

Acknowledging Political Resistance. The political resistance resolution method begins with acknowledging resistance. In other words, identify it. Acknowledging political resistance helps with controlling the emotions associated with differences of opinion, which is critical because arguing and fighting over differences of opinion will accomplish little.

Acknowledging political resistance consists of two activities: listening and sharing. First, you should listen carefully to another person's messages to determine their meaning. Most critical and emotion-laden statements are made to verbalize excess tension or fear. In fact, the very process of listening helps convert tension into words that serve to reduce anxiety, even if the words themselves do not actually reveal the nature of the tension or the reason for it.

The second activity involves sharing of feelings with another person. When you demonstrate your understanding of another person's feelings and are not surprised or upset by negative statements, it illustrates your support, which helps reduce tension. Quite simply, sharing is a form of support. To be successful in this stage, remain calm and neutral, saying and doing nothing that will increase the other person's tensions or fears.

Clarifying Political Resistance. Few people are ready or willing to reveal the reasons for their behavior, even when they understand what they are. They learn to cover up the plausible reasons, justifications, and explanations in an effort to prove that they're acting in a well thought out and logical manner. There is a word that explains this thinking process: rationalization. Therefore, the second step in resolving conflict is to clarify what another person is thinking so they will be prepared to receive new and logical information.

During this phase, the challenge facing you is to make statements lose force without causing people to lose face. Clarifying involves asking nonthreatening questions so that people are allowed to express their thoughts more freely, which clarifies their resistance. By encouraging people to give examples and illustrations, you are helping them grasp their own meaning more clearly. This will help you better understand others' negative statements.

Problem Solving. Once you have clarified a negative statement, you are ready to help people identify solutions to their problems. The problem-solving process typically consists of six steps:

1. Problem identification
2. Political solution identification
3. Political solution analysis
4. Political solution selection
5. Political solution implementation
6. Political solution evaluation

During this phase of the political resistance resolution process, the first four are applicable. The last two are a part of the confirming phase of the political resistance resolution process, which is the last stage of the process.

Problem identification involves analyzing the situation to identify expectations and determine the current situation. The discrepancy between these two positions is the problem. Therefore, the focus of the problem-solving process is finding the "best" political solution to the problem(s).

Identifying political solutions involves generating as many ideas as possible to identify a solution. This activity is conducted without evaluating or examining the ideas. The goal is to come upon with as many possible solutions as possible.

Analyzing political solutions is the process of critically examining each of the possible solutions. Set up criteria to serve as a standard or benchmark by which to filter each idea. Ideas that meet most of the criteria are grouped together for further analysis. The ideas that do not meet the established criteria are filed for future consideration.

Selecting political solutions involves testing the solutions that meet the criteria to decide their practicality and ease of application. Identify the cost and potential results of each solution, which will help you decide the best possible political solution from a cost/benefit perspective.

Another critical part of this phase is to name possible obstacles or barriers that may prevent applying a political solution. As these barriers are identified, look at them and decide the possible effects they have on various solutions. You should identify actions to overcome obstacles or barriers, examining financial, human, and emotional costs. This information will help you decide the best political solution. The outcome of this phase of the problem-solving process is that you have identified the best alternative(s).

Confirming the Answer. When an acceptable political solution has been identified, all parties must make a commitment—typically some kind of immediate action—that reinforces their willingness to accept the remedy. At this time, feedback is essential in evaluating the continuing viability of the solution and of the relationship in general. Finally, the last two phase of the traditional problem-solving process are applicable during this part of the resistance to political resolution process: solution implementation and solution evaluation.

Implementing political solutions is the process of applying the political solution to determine its results. When doing this, you should choose opportunities or situations where the political solution has the highest degree of success. This strategy allows you to integrate the solution under the best possible conditions before they apply it to the entire department, division, or organization.

Implementing political solutions is a slow and deliberate process to give you time to figure out the real outcomes. It is often a good idea to implement a solution in several parts of an organization before introducing it to the entire organization. Then you can refine and redesign the solution as needed.

Ideally, you should gather information and compare results once a political solution has been applied. If the solution helps close the gap between the expectations of the respective parties, it can be considered a success. If, however, the gap remains the same, you may need to consider alternative solutions. Finally, you should document the outcome of every solution advanced and maintain an active record of the dates and location of each. This information will be an invaluable resource for future conflict reduction activities.

Regardless of the outcomes achieved during the political resistance resolution process, the information and knowledge gained is valuable because all parties have participated in a process designed to reduce conflict, which improves relationships, enhances understanding, and facilitates respect among all parties involved. This is a very important outcome of the political resistance resolution method.

PARTNERSHIP SKILLS

Some political engagements falter because they are not based on the needs of the organization and its people (see chapter 6). Others falter because they are not perceived as helping the organization achieve it goals and objectives due to managers' lack of credibility in the organization. There are two reasons for this circumstance. First, some managers fail to demonstrate an understanding of their organization and its business operations, which is evident by the fact that most managers are never invited to participate in discussions regarding the strategic direction of the organization. As a result, organizational leaders do not perceive them as valuable resources. Thus, the organization fails to properly invest in their development. Second, some managers fail to properly communicate the value and benefits of political engagements to others within the organization. Consequently, organizational leaders are unaware of some managers' contributions, and thus, they believe that they are unable to help resolve political conflict. Over time, they view these managers as nonessential in identifying political solutions useful in addressing political conflict. In short, many managers lack political credibility within the organization, hence their career mobility and influence are limited. Political navigators, however, develop partnership skills to overcome these two breakdowns.

Gaining credibility as a political navigator requires demonstrating the knowledge, skills, and abilities that the organization values. It is absolutely prerequisite to solving problems, creating opportunities, capitalizing on strategic opportunities, and leveraging organizational strengths. Partnership skills are essential for you to become proficient in political interactions and engagements. These skills are used to manage political interactions and engagements, deal with political resistance, create interpersonal environments that are conducive to sharing of information, and enlist the support and cooperation of others involved in political interaction and engagements.

Partnership skills are the most eclectic skill sets of a political navigator because they are an integration of the three previously discussed skills (relationship, communication, and conflict resolution). Partnership skills rely on your ability to build and maintain positive synergistic relationships, communicate effectively and clearly, and resolve conflict in a constructive and productive manner. However, you must develop an understanding of partnerships to execute the skills effectively.

By design, a partnership is a long-term, collaborative activity that focuses on achieving results through mutually beneficial relationships used in helping the organization successfully achieve its goals and objectives. These relationships assist you in acquiring a responsive attitude necessary for you to become more people oriented and thereby better understand and anticipate their needs. Partnerships help you decide which political interactions and engagements provide the highest value and have the greatest impact on the organization. They also promote establishment of working relationships based on shared values, aligned purpose and vision, and mutual support. Furthermore, partnerships are based on the business and performance needs of people, not a political navigator's career aspirations or professional success.

Foundations for Partnership Skills

There are two primary elements of partnership skills: purpose and partnering. Purpose brings people together and provides a focus and direction for the partnership, the result of which is clarifying roles and focus. It also embraces underlying assumptions, trust and risk, shared values, and expectations. Purpose defines "why" a partnership is needed. Simply, purpose helps describe what you intend to achieve as a result of a partnership.

Partnering exemplifies the observable dynamics between you and other people engaging in a partnership. It incorporates the common values, beliefs, assumptions, and expectations of all parties in a partnership. Unfortunately, much that is important to partnering often goes unexpressed. Partnering occurs when you and other people pursue a common purpose together. Those who attend to purpose but neglect partnering often fail in their work altogether.

ORGANIZATIONAL UNDERSTANDING SKILLS

Every organization, regardless of its size and complexity, has a political structure and culture that greatly impact its behavior and are necessary to ensure stability and continuity. Employees, managers, and executives adhere to the organization's structure and culture in order to maintain their individual influence. However, the organization's structure and culture are often a major reason why the organization is experiencing political conflict. To compound this situation, it is often difficult for employees and managers to convince organizational decision makers that there is something dysfunctional about the organization. It is not, however, impossible for an objective third party to address such sensitive issues. Under these circumstances it is essential for a manager to serve as political navigator and operate as an advocate for others in the organization.

Political navigators rely on their organizational understanding skills when identifying the needs of all key clients (decision makers, stakeholders, influencers, and scouts) in the organization. Additionally, these skills enable you to identify the issues that ultimately contribute to political conflict in the organization.

Organizational understanding skills can be best demonstrated when you reflect on how organizations work. Simply stated, it is essential for you to think like the people you serve. This understanding requires knowledge of how things get done inside an organization as well as how decisions are made there. Business understanding requires you to have knowledge of business fundamentals, systems theory, organizational culture, and politics. By developing business understanding, you will be better able to facilitate political engagements that help in identifying political solutions that improve organizational effectiveness.

Organizational understanding skills require you to ascertain the readiness and commitment of people to political solutions. The following questions can be used as a guide in this process:

- How willing are the members of the organization to implement political solutions?
- Is upper-level management willing to support political engagements?
- What types of information do members of the organization readily accept or resist?
- What are the members' attitudes toward political solutions?
- What are the executives' attitudes toward political solutions?

Organizational understanding skills also require you to intentionally prioritize the contributions, involvement, and loyalty of people above the organizational system. This is known as organizational subordination. Thus, you demonstrate organizational subordination by eliminating policies and procedures and organizational structures that interfere with, prevent, or discourage the implementation of political solutions.

Organizational understanding skills require you to have the ability to be completely committed to identifying appropriate political solutions. Further, you have the ability to ask others in the organization about their perspective of the organization, its financial and competitive position, strengths and weaknesses, management structure, management capacity, technological state, relationship to competitors, reward and compensation systems used to motivate others, performance appraisal and review systems, performance management system, and management's attitude toward human resources within the organization. These critical areas of inquiry help you acquire an understanding of the organization and the nature of its business and demonstrate your understanding of business fundamentals.

Next, your ability to manage projects (political engagements) is critical. Thus, political navigators possess project management skills that enable them to plan and identify objectives and activities that produce a desired result (political solution), organize people to get the job done and direct them by keeping them focused on achieving the results, and measure the project team's progress and give them feedback to keep the project moving ahead, while constantly monitoring progress toward, and deviation from, the project's goals.

The final organizational understanding skill is systems thinking, which involves viewing and understanding an organization as an open system. Such thinking requires you to have detailed knowledge of the inputs, throughputs, and outputs of the organization, as well as the critical connections and *disconnections* that exist therein. These characteristics form a framework for appraising an organization's internal environment, isolating political problems, and identifying relationships critical to implementing political engagements.

Conducting an Analysis of the Organization and Its Leadership

During this analysis, you evaluate the strengths and weaknesses (internal environment) and the opportunities and threats (external environment) facing the organization. This is commonly known as an S.W.O.T. (Strengths, Weaknesses, Opportunities, and Threats) analysis. It is designed to obtain as much information about the health of an organization as possible. Another purpose of an S.W.O.T. analysis is to identify which contingencies will help an organization carry out its mission and which will hinder it. Based on this analysis, you can help the organization make adjustments that compensate for weaknesses and threats, while at the same time finding ways of help the organization build on strengths and capitalize on political opportunities. Finally, an S.W.O.T. analysis is useful in identifying a wealth of information that will guide you throughout the political engagement process.

Internal Environment. Examination of the internal environment allows for identification of the organization's strengths and weaknesses. This environment obviously affects execution of its mission. A number of areas must be considered when examining the internal environment. Several questions should be asked to determine the strengths and weaknesses of an organization:

1. What is the financial condition of the organization?
2. What are the aptitudes and abilities of managers and employees?
3. What is the current condition of facilities?
4. What is the current state and quality of technology?
5. What is the quantity and quality of material resources?
6. What is the quantity and quality of human resources?
7. What are the current images of various departments and their visions?
8. How is the organization structured?
9. What is the organization's culture?
10. What is the work climate within the organization?
11. What are the policies and procedures that improve or impede organizational performance and effectiveness?
12. What are the managerial practices within the organization?
13. What is the quality of organizational leadership?
14. What are the strengths and weaknesses of the organizational leaders?
15. What are the strengths and weaknesses of the organizational culture?
16. What is the organization's mission and strategy?
17. Does the organization have a formal learning system?
18. What is the compensation and reward system?
19. What is the quality of the performance appraisal process?
20. Is performance coaching used within the organization?

Once these areas have been examined, describe each relationship in terms of its strengths and weaknesses. It is recommended that several data collection methods be used when conducting such an analysis (e. g., interviews, observations, questionnaires, and focus groups). Combining methodologies is an excellent way of ensuring a more accurate picture of the internal state of the organization.

An analysis of the collected data can be used to help you to make recommendations for the improved allocation of material, financial, and human resources in the execution of an organization's goals, objectives, and mission. In so doing, you demonstrate that you have the expertise to analyze the health of your organization, provide recommendations, and provide leadership and guidance that will improve overall effectiveness and efficiency.

External Environment. The long-term conditions facing the organization can be uncovered through an external environmental analysis. Such an analysis identifies and encompasses several important variables, including: resource availability; current economic condition; social and cultural values; the legal and political environment; the organization's competitive rank; performance and organizational gaps, and image in the marketplace.

In order to remain viable in the marketplace, many organizations maintain aggressive research and development programs. An external environmental analysis helps identify the opportunities and threats facing an organization in a given industry, vis-à-vis the amount, type, and quality of technology needed to remain competitive. With the continued escalation of technology, such an analysis will be extremely important to the long-term competitiveness of most organizations and, ultimately, their long-term success. There are a number of questions that are useful in determining the external environment facing an organization:

1. What are the economic conditions of the nation, region, and local community?
2. What social and cultural values predominate within the industry and its geographic locations?
3. What quantity and quality of technology does the organization employ to achieve its business results?
4. What external financial, material, and human resources are available?
5. What is the organization's image in the marketplace?
6. What is the company's competitive rank within the industry?
7. What performance gaps exist within the organization?
8. What organizational effectiveness gaps exist?

This information reveals the economic health of an organization, its values, political climate, use of technology and resources, competitive rank within its industry, overall image, and areas requiring improvement.

Each question provides a wealth of information useful in making decisions regarding the allocation of material, financial, and human resources useful during political engagements. Naturally, such information helps you to make appropriate recommendations and strengthens your credibility in the organization. Once you have identified the opportunities and/or constraints challenging the organization, you are armed with information critical to long-term viability. External analysis also provides information regarding the critical financial and human resources available for expansion and growth. All of this information will help you throughout the political engagement process because it demonstrates that you have the expertise to be an opinion leader in your organization.

When you are able to successfully conduct an S.W.O.T. analysis, you demonstrate that you are a serious political player and can add value to your organization. Additionally, you have a complete and comprehensive understanding of your organization and are in a better position to advocate political solutions that will diminish political conflict.

POLITICAL THINKING SKILLS

All too often, managers react before thinking. Some fail to ask thought-provoking questions but rather ask simple questions that provide little information or understanding behind people's resistance to change. These behaviors can create conditions that ultimately produce poor results, create poor interpersonal relationships, and diminish the success of political interactions.

During any political interaction or engagement, your primary job is to consider what possibilities, circumstances, events, and conditions are creating resistance. You have an obligation to determine why certain political solutions are being fought. Obviously, some political solutions are more appropriate than others; however, you must make certain of this before recommending and implementing them. To that end, you take the time to observe others; identify other people's needs, interests, expectations, and opinions; examine historical documents reflect on past political interactions; interview interested parties; solicit input from others; and identify a list of questions to be asked before participating in political interactions and engagements. The ultimate purpose of gathering this type of information is to have meaning and purposeful conversations, garner support, make informed decisions, and provide acceptable recommendations. In short, the solution is to think politically, continually asking others about themselves, their opinions, ideas, suggestions, and recommendations. When this approached is used, political navigators are using political thinking skills.

Political thinking skills can include a number of behaviors:

- thinking before reacting
- listening carefully and selectively to others' requests during political interactions
- filtering suggestions and recommendations through a defined philosophy of interpersonal relationships
- understanding one's role during political interactions and engagements
- possessing the courage to encourage political solutions that are appropriate but not popular

- analyzing all requests as requests rather than as commands
- maintaining consistent guiding principles to ensure credibility

By constantly exploring and asking questions, you are not focusing on the status quo, but are continuously looking for new and improved ways of enhancing your relationships with other people and the effectiveness of the organization. Consequently, political thinking is as much a state of mind as it is a series of techniques and processes. Political navigators who are continually examining the state of others and the organization and comparing it with an ideal vision are constantly in touch with the problems and issues facing the people and the organization.

CONCLUSION

To become a political navigator, you need to develop several critical skills to facilitate and manage political interactions and engagements and to implement political solutions. Each of these competencies positively improves organizational effectiveness. Acquiring this expertise is a time-consuming and complex process; however, once obtained, it will enhance your credibility and influence in the organization.

REFERENCES

Block, Peter. *Flawless Consulting: A Guide to Getting Your Expertise Used.* 2d. ed. San Diego: Pfeiffer, 1999.

Merrill, David, and Richard Reid. *Personality Styles and Effective Performance.* Radnor, PA: Chilton, 1981.

FIVE

Strategies for Political Navigators

The complex nature of politics forces you to draw upon a multitude of skills and abilities to successfully maneuver through and manage organizational obstacles and opportunities. Returning to the bicycle metaphor introduced in chapter 1, these skills and abilities encompass both "front wheel" and "back wheel" competencies that are required to establish credibility.

In this chapter, the strategies for improving power, politics, and influence in organizations will be examined. The strategies represent ways of improving your effectiveness, capacity, and capability as a political navigator. Individually, each strategy can improve your credibility, but collectively, they can transform you into a sophisticated, thoughtful, articulate, and polished political player. Using these strategies will help you achieve results and outcomes while building and maintaining collaborative working relationships.

Several strategies can be used to improve your political savvy. They are cluster into four primary types. They include: preparation, protection, effectiveness, and competency strategies.

PREPARATION STRATEGIES

Preparation strategies are those that are used in anticipation of political interactions and engagements. They are designed to provide you the most solid foundation possible. They are also useful in establishing a macro understanding of one's organization, its people, political environment, the political dynamics that exist within the organization, conflict management styles used by members of the organization, and any other important information that needs to be considered so that you can be an effective political navigator.

Observing, Observing, Observing

Pay attention to your environment, especially to the interactions between people and the patterns of these interactions. By doing so, you will gather a wealth of information to make important decisions and avoid political landmines. Observation requires you to identify connections between people and groups so that you can approach political interactions and engagements in an informed manner. Effective political navigators spend far more time observing than communicating. It could be said that effective political interactions and engagements are more about what you see than what you do. Furthermore, observation allows you to examine the political terrain prior to engaging in a political interaction and engagement. Observation also allows you the opportunity to gather your thoughts, reflect on current and past events, draw conclusions, and formulate strategies while others are busy formulating and executing political maneuvers.

Identifying the Power

Chapter 2 identified several different sources of interpersonal power and functional power. You should rely on these sources as you prepare for political interactions or engagements. This includes determining who in the organization has the power to make decisions and get things done and identifying those individuals who have access to powerful individuals. Whenever possible you should use the integrative perspective of power, because it creates a win-win scenario for all parties and helps improve communications, enhances cooperation, and creates synergy (see chapter 2). Once power has been identified, you create a strategy for creating and/ or maintaining positive relationships with all parties while also achieving specific results and outcomes.

Developing Integration Skills

Political navigators are able to examine a political situation, dissect it into various elements, and determine and explain the relationships between and among people. Further, political navigators have the ability to develop linkages between people who implement political engagements or manage and deal with resistance during political interactions; create work environments that are conducive for sharing of information; and enlist the support and cooperation of organizational leaders, advocates, and team members during political interactions and engagements. Political navigators have the ability to remain impartial regardless of personal loyalties, values, or biases, and in spite of an organization's culture, corporate traditions, or vested interests. This impartiality is perhaps is the greatest single benefit that you can provide.

Building Coalitions Tied to the Organization's Grapevine

Building a coalition is a process by which you develop a network of contacts throughout the organization. Coalition building provides you an opportunity to partner with people who can provide advice, introductions, and assistance, which can substantially enhance your political influence. However, the organizational "grapevine" is often viewed as an unavoidable threat to one's political success. Far too many managers approach the grapevine as something that they must react to after political damage has been done.

Political navigators understand the power and influence of a political coalition. They realize that such a coalition has great potential for a win-win outcome. One of the benefits of such networks is that you help others achieve more "formal" credibility among their peers by providing them with official information in advance of anyone else. In fact, you can eliminate many conflicts by partnering with those individuals who have the potential to be the primary barrier during political interactions and engagements. In turn, these individuals can serve as your closest and most immediate sensors for what the moods and emotions are among the rest of the people in the organization at any given phase of a political engagement (see chapter 6). Building a coalition of such individuals enables them to be part of the solution rather than being part of the problem.

Developing Contacts in the Organization

A closely related activity to building a coalition is developing contacts in an organization. Here you engage in overt efforts to develop rapport with people who can help you succeed in the organization. In most cases, this is a long-term strategy that requires building a broad network of contacts. Since this is a long-term strategy, it is critical that you begin developing such contacts immediately upon your arrival in organization (or new department, division, or unit of the organization).

One of the best ways to develop contacts in organization is to a technique known as referral. Developing referrals is a process by which you ask other individuals to introduce you to influential people in the organization. This can include individuals at your current level in the organization as well as those at higher levels. The purpose of this activity is to guarantee that you know as many people in the organization as possible and have individuals that you can go to during politically difficult times. A secondary purpose is to cultivate contacts with people who can make introductions on your behalf to others in the organization. This may be invaluable to you in the future.

Keeping Your Powder Dry

During the flintlock era of military history, *keeping your powder dry* reminded soldiers to always make certain that their gunpowder was free of moisture so that they could engage the enemy at a moment's notice. In our context, keeping your powder dry refers to maintaining readiness for political action. In other words, never take things for granted and be ready to engage in political activities at the first sign of trouble. Further, always be prepared for any unseen contingency or opportunity during political interactions and engagements. Accordingly, political navigators are always on guard and are never complacent with the circumstances surrounding them. Remember, many of your political adversaries are waiting for an opportunity to spring a surprise attack on you and overwhelm you politically. Always be on guard for the unknown.

Building Rapport with the "Right People"

Make connections with people who are able to grant you permission to participate in high-profile political interactions and engagements. Such individuals should have access to senior managers and decision makers in an organization. These people should be willing to support and protect you during unfriendly and heated political interactions and engagements as well as provide you advice, recommendations, and suggestions for how to proceed. Is critically important that you have respect for these individuals and can trust them explicitly, otherwise you will always wonder whether they have your best interest at heart.

If you have properly built a coalition and made appropriate contacts in the organization, you should have access to the "right people." Otherwise, is impossible to establish rapport or gain access to such individuals during a new political engagement. In other words, you must be proactive in the execution of this strategy. This is not a strategy that can be implemented unless the appropriate groundwork has been laid. Most importantly, you should make certain that the relationship you have with such individuals is genuine, sincere, and mutually beneficial. This will ensure that you have developed rapport for the right reasons. Accordingly, you will develop very powerful and influential allies.

Embracing Your Worst Political Adversary as a Human Being

Befriend your political enemies so that you can discover mutual ground from which to build a working relationship. While this may appear to be a very distasteful activity, it has proven to be a very effective and rewarding strategy. It is not uncommon for former political adversaries to become enthusiastic allies but this cannot occur unless you are willing to engage the individuals who are presently your political adversaries.

You can employ this strategy by first identifying characteristics that you have in common with a political adversary. By identifying common characteristics, you are identifying areas that you can work on together. This should provide you with common ground from which to build a collaborative relationship. Additionally, you should identify values and beliefs that you have in common. This provides a greater understanding of the other person and should lessen your hostility and disdain for that individual.

Developing Favor Banks

Doing favors for others is much like making a deposit in a savings account. Over time, the principal and interest grow to a point where you can cash in and take advantage of an opportunity. This strategy is as much of an attitude as it is an action. In other words, being willing to do favors for others demonstrates your sincere interest and concern for people. In chapter 2, responsiveness to the needs and expectations of people was identified as one of the vital dimensions necessary for becoming a political navigator. Such responsiveness reflects your sincere interest and concern for people and can be demonstrated when you are willing to provide favors for others.

Some mistakenly think that providing favors means providing extraordinary service or efforts that will indebt another person to you forever.

This is simply not the case. Providing favors is simply the thoughtful things that you should be doing for people every day. They require little or no effort on your part but they do demonstrate your willingness to be concerned about other people's needs and expectations. This strategy cuts through the entire pretense and exposes your true intentions and meaning. In short, providing favors for other people demonstrates that you are simply a nice, sincere, and caring person.

Knowing the Strengths/Weaknesses of Your Conflict Management Style

Chapter 2 introduced five conflict management styles. Each of the styles has its strengths and weaknesses, and it is imperative that you know what they are. This will enable you to build on your strengths while managing your weaknesses. In this way, you will continue to maximize the things that you do well and avoid the things that can get you in trouble. Further, knowing your strengths and weaknesses demonstrates that you are making every attempt to function as a politically conscious competent.

A conscious competent person spends time reflecting on events and activities to gain new knowledge and insight. Armed with this awareness, you are less likely to repeat inappropriate political behavior or make serious political mistakes in the future. This strategy will help protect your credibility by maintaining consistent and unified behavior during all political interactions and engagements.

PROTECTION STRATEGIES

As you engage in political interactions and initiate political engagements, it is critical that you identify strategies that help protect you during such events. These are known as protection strategies and are vital to your mental well-being as well as your political success. They are designed to provide political cover and defense during the heat of political interactions and engagements. Each of the strategies will help you be more assertive because you have the confidence that you have strategies that will give you a distinct advantage during political conflicts.

Being Nice and Friendly

Be nice and friendly to people who otherwise do not care for you; sometime in the future they will notice and reciprocate the behavior. People are drawn to those people who reach out and appear to be open and warm. Furthermore, this strategy is important because you never know when an individual that you currently interact with might be plucked up by management and placed in a position of extreme power and influence.

Throughout this book, the importance of developing collaborative, synergistic relationships has been emphasized. This is done in an attempt to communicate the importance of establishing relationships that are beneficial and contribute to your political success. Therefore, being nice and friendly seems to be the prerequisite to building such relationships. In fact, you will never become a political navigator unless people perceive you as someone who is approachable, respectful, receptive, and pleasant.

Picking Your Battles

It is critically important that you select carefully the political battles on which you are willing to spend precious emotional capital. Avoid the "combat ready" approach that diminishes your energy and effectiveness. Further, you do not want to be known as the type of individual in an organization who is always engaged in disagreements and/or conflicts. You should make certain that you spend your political capital wisely. This is done by selecting only those political engagements that provide you the opportunity to enhance your credibility and influence in the organization (see chapter 6).

Individuals who are known as contrarians are perceived as difficult, unapproachable, and mean-spirited. You want to avoid these types of labels whenever possible. Therefore, select the issues that you are willing to stake your influence and credibility on and engage in those battles in an enthusiastic and assertive manner. Finally, it is essential that you pick political battles that threaten your values and beliefs because these are the more essential to your identity, self-esteem, and personal worth.

Utilizing the Crazy Person Strategy

One of the most controversial strategies that you can employ is what I call the *crazy person strategy*. Examples of this behavior include: raising your voice; standing up and walking out of the room; looking intently into someone else's eyes, not saying a word; leaning forward in your chair with your elbows on the table; providing a rapid-fire series of aggressive, focused, and direct questions designed to prevent another person from responding while increasing your vocal intensity as you ask each question; intently shaking your head while batting your eyes quickly; and making statements such as "enough is enough." What you are doing is demonstrating behaviors that are typically uncharacteristic for you. This strategy is used to shock your opponent, which gives you a distinct advantage during political interactions or engagements. Another reason to use this technique is to demonstrate your intensity, passion, assertiveness, and personal will to prevent aggressive people from attacking you or undermining the political situations that you recommend. The technique is used to make certain that individuals and groups realize that pushing you into positions or forcing you to make decisions that are inappropriate will result in a rather explosive display of human behavior. In other words, this technique is used to send a message that you are a formidable opponent and messing with you will come at a very high price. One note of caution, *this strategy should be used very infrequently.*

This strategy is demonstrated every day in the wildernesses around the world. For example, one of the most aggressive animals in nature is a North American badger or wolverine. Weighing less than 35 pounds, this intense, focused, and territorial animal is seldom attacked by much larger animals such as grizzly bears, coyotes, and timber wolves. The primary reason that such predators avoid wolverines is because they will inflict serious injury upon their opponent if attacked. On the other hand, wolverines seldom are the aggressors toward larger animals. This is nature's way of demonstrating that animals willing to protect themselves are seldom attacked, which is an excellent metaphor for illustrating this important political strategy.

I believe it is important for people to realize that you are willing to stand up for yourself rather than be taken advantage of and pushed around. When other people realize that you have "an edge" to your personality, they are more reluctant to exercise excessive force when interacting with you regardless of how powerful they are in the organization. It is also important to remember that you should never be the aggressor during a political interaction or engagement: assertiveness, yes; aggressiveness, no.

For some of you, demonstrating this strategy will be very difficult because you do not have an assertive personality. If this is the case, one suggestion is to pretend that you are playing a role that requires you to act more assertively than normal. This will encourage you to act more assertively and demonstrate that there is a point where you will no longer tolerate heavy-handed politics and inappropriate political behavior.

Knowing When to Fold Them

Sometimes you are outnumbered or do not have the support needed to successfully accomplish your goals. Thus, the strategy of knowing when to fold them reminds you that it is sometimes better to avoid a conflict than a suffer a humiliating defeat. Initiate a graceful retreat under these conditions and live to fight another day, hopefully under better and more manageable circumstances. Further, this strategy helps you make appropriate political decisions by preventing you from taking unnecessary and foolish risks. It reminds you that political success is dependent upon positive and effective partnerships, allies, and supporters that are willing to engage in political actions for the benefit of several constituent groups in an organization. When you have overextended yourself, misinterpreted the situation, or underestimated your competition, this strategy is appropriate in helping you maintain your credibility by preventing political miscalculations.

Keeping Your Distance

Sometimes getting too close to others in the organization is counterproductive. Share just enough of yourself to be effective; never get too intimately involved with people who can affect your career and livelihood. This may be a difficult strategy for those who are very people oriented and desire strong relationships with others at work.

This strategy requires you to balance relationships in such a way that you do not put yourself in a situation where you can be taken advantage of by others. Furthermore, it is sometimes advantageous for others to wonder about your background, experiences, and personality. People are sometimes negatively biased when they know too much about you, which can limit your political influence and effectiveness.

Demonstrating Poise

We are all familiar with the catchphrase "do not let them see you sweat." Demonstrating poise is effective because it is designed to reassure people that you are a competent, experienced, and seasoned political player. For example, during a very intense political interaction, people's emotions eventually rise to the surface, tempers flare, things are said, and outbursts are witnessed. However, if you remain perfectly calm during turbulent political events, it will demonstrate that you are a calming force that can be relied on under pressure. Controlling your emotions also allows you to focus on the issues, facts, ideas, and other people's comments and suggestions.

Another reason for remaining calm is that other people will not realize how important the issue is to you. Therefore, they will not know your true intentions, giving you an advantage during negotiations. This might be the leverage that you need in order to obtain the results and outcomes you desire. Finally, this strategy enables you to maintain positive relationships with all parties by demonstrating your concerns for people and their needs.

Avoiding Public Confrontations

Never allow yourself to engage in public displays of aggressiveness or hostility. Always confront others in private and do so in a tactful, intelligent manner. This strategy will help you maintain a professional image under fire. Public confrontations are simply inappropriate political behavior. It demonstrates your lack of emotional control and communicates lack of professionalism. If public confrontations occur, they create long-term resentment and hurt feelings that can seldom be overcome. Finally, they are an embarrassment to both you and your constituents, and they can seriously jeopardize the results and outcomes you desire.

EFFECTIVENESS STRATEGIES

Effectiveness strategies refer to those activities that are used during political interactions and engagements that give you a differential advantage. They are designed to help you facilitate communications and achieve desired results and outcomes. Typically, they are strategies that help you make decisions under pressure that improve your credibility and influence in the organization. Finally, they are strategies that are proactive and help you maneuver under difficult circumstances.

Doing the Unexpected

Do things that others do not expect. This includes demonstrating talents, abilities, and skills that others are not familiar with. In this way, you become a mystery to others, which can increase their interest in you as a person and as a professional. During the unexpected also includes adopting tactics that others have not seen you display in the past. This can include such things as supporting recommendations that are not consistent with your pattern of behavior and identify alternatives that you have not supported previously. The primary purpose of this strategy is to keep people guessing as to your behavior, actions, and decisions. In this way, you are unpredictable and therefore less controllable.

Advocating Solutions

Advocating solutions requires you to influence individuals to choose particular actions or solutions that resolve conflict. This strategy requires you to be very directive, proactive, and persuasive. It could be said that political navigators are "selling" organizational leaders and others during this activity.

Providing Objective Observations

Objective observation is a non-directive activity that enables you to witness the effects that political interactions and engagements have on people and helps you guide them in their effort to overcome their resistance to new ideas, innovations, and discoveries.

Guarding against Complacency

This strategy implies that you should never take anything for granted. This includes relationships, connections, and how others perceive you. Always enter the political arena believing that you are behind and must play harder and smarter than the other people. This strategy also encourages you to engage in the activities that have enabled you to function as a political navigator. As such, you demonstrate that you have not forgotten the hard work, dedication, and discipline required to achieve this level of credibility and influence in organization. Guarding against complacency also reminds you that nothing is certain and that you must continue to work hard and be dedicated to achieving appropriate results and outcomes while building and maintaining positive, collaborative, synergistic relationships.

Securing the High Ground

This strategy helps you identify when conditions are right to initiate a political engagement or seek support for a political solution. *Securing the high ground* is an old military slogan used to communicate a competitive advantage over the enemy. Ancient armies that were able to secure the high ground had a distinct advantage over their adversaries. Throughout history, less superior armies that secured the high ground almost always defeated superior armies. During political interactions and engagements, securing the high ground refers to having a competitive advantage over your adversaries. This could include having support from individuals who are influential and powerful within the organization or having prepared a more logical and rational recommendation for action. Finally, this strategy includes understanding the importance of securing powerful relationships and partnerships as well as having a well-thought-out plan for executing political strategies (see chapter 6).

Developing Finesse

Create a polished and professional approach to playing smart politics. This involves studying others who have mastered the art of political gamesmanship. The greater your political sophistication, the more credible you will become as a political player. In some ways this is the ultimate preparation strategy because a sophisticated, poised, polished, and articulate political navigator is a force to be reckoned with, regardless of who the political adversary might be.

Thinking Like a Chess Player

There are very few games that require more advanced thinking than playing chess. It requires you to envision the game several moves ahead and to anticipate your opponent's every move. Politically competent individuals are adept at learning the lay of the land so they can set about creating the conditions that will ensure that their efforts are successful. This strategy answers the question "what am I up against?" (see chapter 6).

Thinking like a chess player requires you to identify coalitions, solicit opinions, and observe connections before you offer your opinions. This will require you to spend valuable time observing and evaluating others, which includes their values, belief, behaviors, and tendencies.

Playing It Close to the Vest

You should share just enough information so that other people support and open doors for you. Never let others know everything you are thinking and feeling. Like playing poker, never show another player your cards. If you do, they have the advantage.

Previously, we discussed a strategy known as keeping your distance, which refers to your interpersonal interactions with other people. The play it close to the vest technique is not interpersonal in nature but is a tactical activity. In other words, this technique encourages you not to share important information, solutions, recommendations, and actions openly during political interactions and engagements. Identical to your distance strategy, this tactic encourages you to remain guarded and reserved with the information that you share with others. This guarantees that only you know strategies that you are going to execute, which prevents others from developing strategies that counteracted your actions.

Standing Your Ground

You must be willing to fight vigorously for important, value-based issues. Such issues are worth expending your political capital. Remember that political aggressors will avoid you like most animals avoid the small but tenacious wolverine—they understand that a serious confrontation with such an animal is just too painful. This strategy communicates that you are ready, willing, and able to engage in assertive political behavior, if necessary. You must avoid unnecessary compromises that undermine your position. Accepting and supporting unfounded and poorly thought out recommendations and actions will only weaken your future support. Strong adversaries respect strength and disdain weakness. Therefore, it is better for you to "fight the good fight" than to surrender and demonstrate vulnerability.

Impeccable Timing

One of the most difficult strategies to teach or acquire is a sense of timing. It is sometimes referred to as a *sixth sense* that guides your thinking and actions, prevents you from making serious mistakes, and allows you to take advantage of situations. Timing requires you to pay attention to the environment and people around you as well as maintain an awareness of your own mental, physical, and spiritual condition.

Many of the world's great military battles and sporting events have turned as a result of someone's impeccable sense of timing. This is because great leaders have an intuitive feel that guides their behavior and action. Some believe that this skill cannot be developed because it an inherent ability; however, most individuals can improve their sense of timing by realizing that in every political interaction and engagement there will be a moment that changes the course of events forever. Consequently, you must plan for that moment by anticipating it and developing strategies and contingency plans accordingly.

Another way of looking at impeccable timing is to implement the following slogan: "pick your spot." This refers to developing strategies and implementing actions when you are at maximum strength politically and your opponent is either unprepared for or not aware of your next action(s). In essence, you have taken advantage of a leverage point in the political interactions and engagement that gives you the advantage. Exploit that advantage and win the day.

Balancing Results and Relationships

It is critical that you balance concerns for people with a desire to achieve results. Politically savvy individuals understand the importance of responding to senior management's concerns for results while making certain that the needs and expectations of people are met. In chapter 2, we refer to individuals who balance both results and relationships in such a way as to satisfy all constituent groups as having a conflict management style known as that of political navigator.

As discussed in chapter 1, political interactions are one-on-one and small-group exchanges that allow you the opportunity to build rapport with others while simultaneously achieving small but important results. On the other hand, political engagements are complicated and complex set of actions design to achieve wholesale results. This macro activity also has a relationship component woven throughout the process. However, the principal purpose of a political engagement is to achieve significant, sweeping, and comprehensive results without jeopardizing relationships (see chapter 6).

Accordingly, some solutions are both highly effective in solving problems and highly effective politically. More likely than not, solutions are trade-offs between results and relationships. It is incumbent upon you to focus your energies on identifying solutions that can maximize results while building and maintaining strong relationships. This requires you to be very effective during political interactions (chapter 1) and political engagements (chapter 6). In combination, these critical processes are used to achieve results while building and maintaining relationships.

Thinking on Your Feet

During political interactions and engagements, it is important that you maintain your composure and the ability to think on your feet. Most of us have occasions where we have thought of important things to say immediately after a meeting or exchange with another person. You think "these were excellent retorts and insightful comebacks," but unfortunately, they were never shared. What a missed opportunity. One of the reasons that we fail to express ourselves "in the moment" is because we are caught up in an *egocentric predicament*. Psychologists tell us that this condition is one in which we consciously disengaged because we are thinking about other events and how we might respond to them. To illustrate this point, conduct the following exercise: Hand out a letter or memo to a group of people; assign each person a paragraph to read out loud, and instruct someone to begin reading. After two of the paragraphs have been read, ask the person who is responsible for reading the third paragraph to summarize the first two paragraphs.

In most cases, the person will be unable to summarize the content, substance, or purpose of the each of the first two paragraphs. Why? This is because they are engaged in an egocentric predicament as explained previously. This is the primary reason that we are unable to think on our feet during political interactions and it can have a devastating effect.

Thinking on your feet requires complete concentration and focus. Further, you must anticipate what another person is about to say, ask, or do and have appropriate responses to counteract their statements and actions.

You must also pay attention to your physiological state. Sweaty palms and shortness of breath are indicators that you are not relaxed and composed, which is essential to be during political interactions and engagements. You will need to discover ways of relaxing during interpersonal exchanges so that you can be more effective.

Asking Well-Placed Reflective Questions

Many people mistakenly believe that only assertive individuals are persuasive. This is simply not the case. Reflective and thoughtful people are just as effective at persuading others as those who dominate conversations. In fact, the ability to ask well-placed reflective questions is often more effective than well-thought-out and articulate arguments. When solving problems, you ask reflective questions and help people clarify or alter their perspective on a given political situation. Thus, you serve as verifier and philosopher by asking reflective questions that improve the quality of political interactions and engagements.

Asking questions demonstrates that you are interested in what another person is saying and are making every effort to accept their opinion and logic. When you encourage another person to share their ideas, opinions, and thoughts, you are enhancing their self-esteem. Therefore, asking reflective questions could be considered an interpersonal relationship building strategy for enhancing rapport between you and the other person.

Another reason for asking well-placed reflective questions is that doing so gives you an opportunity to think. In other words, it buys you time to develop an effective response to another person's statements. Reflective questions are also an effective technique in guiding and directing the conversation. Such questions can provide structure to a conversation, allowing you to gather a great deal of information in a very short period of time. Reflective questions allow you to expend your energy in small increments while verbal communications can be exhausting. This can sometimes be a differential advantage during long protracted political interactions.

Letting It Go

After emotion-laden and heated political interactions and engagements, it is important to simply "let it go." This means that you should dismiss and disregard such events so that you can focus on more important priorities. While it is important to reflect upon such events and activities so that you can gain insight and understanding, it can be counterproductive to dwell on them for extended periods of time, especially if the outcomes were negative. You can do precious little about past events; therefore, you should spend the majority of your time and energy focusing on future activities. In this way, you are becoming a proactive rather than a reactive political navigator.

COMPETENCY STRATEGIES

Competency strategies are used to demonstrate the skills, knowledge, and abilities political navigators need when engaging in political interactions and engagements. Chapter 4 identified several critical competencies of political navigators. These are the essential skills that are necessary for you to be politically successful in your organization. These competencies consist of both "front wheel" and "back wheel" expertise and require considerable effort to master. Let's examine some strategies that were not addressed in that chapter that will provide you additional insight and awareness.

Creating a Thirty-Second Commercial

Effective political navigators quickly and effectively communicate their mission, purpose, goals, objectives, and the value of their activities, services, and expertise. This is done to demonstrate professional competence in the organization and remind others of professional expertise.

One way of promoting yourself is to create a short, concise, but thorough message—a "thirty-second commercial"—about yourself, your areas of expertise, and your experience. This commercial is shared with interested and curious individuals throughout your organization. Further, this message communicates the advantages, benefits, and value of your expertise, experience, and insight.

An effective thirty-second message includes your professional background and outcomes that you helped the organization achieve. It also touches on the special way that you work with others in the organization to realize those outcomes. While this is a great deal of information to work into thirty seconds, it is important to communicate as much of this information in as brief and memorable a manner as possible. An alternative approach would be to create a series of thirty-second commercials that can be used to promote each of the previously identified topic areas (i.e., background, experience, expertise, collaborative working relationships), so that you can communicate the most appropriate message to whomever the audience happens to be. Keeping the message short prevents information overload. The most important message to be communicated reveals the value that you bring to the organization and how your expertise helps the organization achieve its operational outcomes. Such a message is the centerpiece of the thirty-second commercial strategy.

Identifying with Clients

This strategy includes identifying with clients' interests and expectations, business customs and behavior, dress and manners, and speech and language. You must be willing to communicate with clients at their level by using terminology with which clients relate. The principal advantage of this strategy is that it is the fastest way of building a relationship with a client. Further, communicate using terms that clients value, such as *return on investment, profitability, operational results, cost-effectiveness, improved efficiency, quality performance,* or *revenue enhancements.* These simple terms help demonstrate your awareness of their critical business issues.

Practicing Reciprocity

By treating people the way they want to be treated, you are practicing reciprocity. Hopefully, others will reciprocate like behavior. This strategy is based on a philosophy that if you treat another person with dignity and respect, he or she will typically treat you in a similar manner. Further, reciprocity demonstrates a humble attitude and conciliatory spirit.

Developing Mutual Interests with Clients

Through self-disclosure or using open-ended questions that search out and highlight common history, ideas, and experiences, you are able to gain valuable insights into the interests of your clients. Third-party references also provide an excellent way to identify mutual interests. This technique identifies a common experience or mutual acquaintance. The process is not designed to trick clients or develop a superficial relationship with them; it is a genuine attempt to explore commonality.

Becoming a Scout

As a *scout,* you operate as a visionary within the organization, guiding the organization through uncharted territory in the quest for improvement and maneuvering through obstacles, seeking viable paths. You lead the organization into areas it has not gone before by providing an understanding of internal and external future events, trends, and relationships. As a scout, you prioritize, generate innovative solutions to complex problems, synthesize other people's input, direct the organization toward achieving its business goals, and translate these into action plans. Of course, this cannot occur without developing a well-honed understanding of business operations, systems theory, and financial management.

Becoming a Strategic Partner

As a *strategic partner,* you communicate benefits of political interactions and engagements. Strategic partners understand the critical factors affecting organizational competitiveness and possess a thorough understanding of core processes, operations, business fundamentals, and procedures.

Strategic partners unify a myriad of divisions, departments, units, and functions to work in harmony to achieve efficient, effective business results. Strategic partners are aligned to a common set of guiding principles that provide their purpose, define the organization's direction, and focus. As such, you help members of the organization pull in the same direction to achieve a common set of business results. Your effectiveness is measured by the ability to communicate the value and importance of teamwork and establish connections between departments.

Becoming an Influencer

As an *influencer,* you are direct in your attempt to influence people's thinking, initiate political interaction and engagements, or provide specific recommendations that address complex political problems. To be successful as an influencer, you guard against your own personal biases and strong opinions while remaining receptive to others' views, ideas, and recommendations. You encourage the organization to take risks to achieve its goals and objectives.

Becoming a Strategist

As a *strategist,* you are competent in assessing organizational needs using quantitative and qualitative methodologies. Strategists incorporate the ideas of others into action plans and develop and execute political interactions and engagements that are critical to the success of the organization and promote your credibility and influence. You also evaluate the effectiveness of political interactions and engagements on overall organizational effectiveness.

Becoming a Problem Solver

As a *problem solver,* you strive to assess which perceived problems are critical to the organization. You take an active role in the decision making and engage in political interactions and engagements that reduce conflict so that the organization can operate more efficiently and effectively. As such, you spend a majority of your time helping people make decisions that are beneficial to achieving desired results.

Becoming a Communicator

From the beginning, an effective relationship is a collaborative search for acceptable answers to your clients' real needs and concerns. Ideally, this will be a mutually beneficial relationship. Becoming an effective communicator helps you accomplish this goal as well as to develop trust with your clients. Trust will increase clients' readiness to accept political solutions, suggestions, and recommendations that resolve conflict.

Becoming a Collaborator

Political navigators establish credibility and gain people's confidence to implement political interaction by becoming collaborators. As a *collaborator*, you tailor communications to your audience, listen and ask appropriate questions, engage in informal communications that build support, present ideas clearly and concisely through well-organized written and interpersonal communications, and identify commonalties among various groups to determine shared interests.

Improving Client Relationships through Learning

As a political navigator, it is essential that you establish positive working relationships with clients. Such relationships are the basis of all political interactions and engagements. Several activities can help you become a competent relationship builder. These include turning assertions into questions, giving clients options, making meetings and reports meaningful, helping clients implement solutions and interventions, being accessible, and always, always adding value.

One of the best ways of improving client relationships is helping clients learn. In this way clients develop the knowledge and skills needed for adjusting to future conditions, addressing future problems, and implementing change. Learning will enhance clients' self-esteem, which in turn will help improve your relationship with them. You can also facilitate client learning by helping clients develop critical thinking skills. These skills will help clients improve their professional practice, resulting in better approaches to accomplishing work. However, client learning must be linked to the organization's strategic business goals and objectives in order to be of lasting value.

CONCLUSION

Becoming a political navigator requires you to practice strategies that help you prepare for political interactions and engagements. Adopt strategies that will protect you during political interactions and improve your effectiveness during political engagements. Finally, you need to develop strategies that demonstrate your competence as a political navigator.

As a political navigator, you frame arguments in terms of organizational goals while developing the right image. Gain control of organizational resources, make yourself appear indispensable, and be visible throughout the organization. Next, develop powerful allies and avoid "tainted" members whenever possible. Finally, support organizational leaders whenever possible.

SIX

Political Engagements: Playing to Win

There is no such thing as a neat, well-mannered, war. The same is true during political engagements. If someone is preventing you from achieving your professional goals and you decide to confront them, play to win. While this appears to be simple, straightforward advice, many fail to heed it. When engaging in political activities, few people recognize the seriousness of the situation, and therefore do not engage with appropriate force and aggressiveness. They are quickly overwhelmed by superior forces and have to make a hasty retreat in order to survive politically.

Many individuals simply do not have the heart to take on their political adversaries. They mistakenly live under the delusion that their political adversaries mean no harm through their political action and behavior. All too often these individuals fail to recognize that their political adversary's objective is to destroy their political effectiveness, devastate their career, and/or run them out of the organization. Regardless, you are at war and you must take evasive action to survive, but more importantly, you must engage your political adversaries in such a way as to gain political advantage. In the final analysis, you must destroy your political adversaries or they will destroy you.

During the battle of Pearl Harbor, the Japanese failed to initiate a third and final wave of attack. They did not realize that they had utterly and completely destroyed American air cover over Pearl Harbor during the first two waves of attack. Consequently, the Americans were virtually defenseless to further Japanese attack and another attack could have dealt the U.S. Navy a history-altering defeat. Instead the Japanese navy withdrew, satisfied with its apparent victory.

Why did the Japanese navy make this severe military mistake? After their first two waves of attack, Admiral Yamamoto was reluctant to further engage the U.S. Navy because he had lost the element of surprise and was afraid of an American counterattack. Unfortunately, he did not realize his strategic and superior military advantage. Thus, he did not order a final assault on the Americans. If he had realized his superior position, he could have changed the course of World War II. His inaction allowed the Americans to live to fight another day. His famous quote at the conclusion of the battle was: "I'm afraid that all we've done is awakened a sleeping giant and filled it with great resolve." History proved that to be the case.

EIGHT PHASES OF POLITICAL ENGAGEMENTS

The previous example is a classic illustration of engaging the enemy in battle and allowing them to live to fight another day. Political engagements are much like military campaigns in that they have distinct phases of execution. Both include investigation, analysis, coalition building, strategy, execution and implementation, and evaluation that determines the extent of success or failure.

Figure 6.1 outlines the eight phase of a political engagement. Each phase is distinctive and is dependent upon the other for success. You cannot bypass any of the phases and they must be followed in the prescribed order. This process requires that you use each of the skills discussed in chapter 4. These include relationship, communication, conflict resolution, partnership, organizational understanding, and political thinking skills. Political engagements are designed to enhance your credibility and influence if you can successfully resolve the political conflict.

The political engagement process begins with identifying and defining the political crisis that has emerged. Analyze the situation to identify expectations and determine the differentiation between what you have and what you need. The discrepancy between these two positions is the political crisis facing you in the organization. The focus of the political engagement process is to find the best solution to the political crisis. During this process, identify proper solutions and actions designed to close the gap between the current and desired state.

Political engagements consist of clearly defined phases. Each phase is designed to accomplish specific objectives that lead to a positive conclusion. The first three phases address four specific questions. They are as follows:

1. What am I up against?
2. What is the organization's DNA?
3. How do I raise visibility and create a sense of urgency?
4. What partnerships must be established to guarantee success?

Accordingly, the first two questions help you appraise the situation, determine the characteristics and components of your organization, and examine the strengths and weaknesses of the organization and its management. The third question leads you to formulating strategies that help you create a sense of urgency regarding the political conflict. The fourth question helps you identify strategies for establishing credibility and relationships essential to the successful execution of a political engagement. Consequently the first three phases of the political engagement process are:

Phase 1: Surveying the landscape (this addresses questions 1 and 2)
Phase 2: Creating a sense of urgency (this addresses question 3)
Phase 3: Creating political partnerships (this addresses question 4)

The next two phases of the political engagement process address three specific questions. They are as follows:

1. What are the possible political solutions for resolving the political conflict?
2. What is the best solution to resolving the political conflict?
3. What are the foundational principles for implementing political solutions?

These three questions help you identify strategies and principles appropriate for identifying, selecting, and implementing a political solution. Further, they force you to critically analyze the situation and develop a plan of action dedicated to success. These two phases of the political engagement process are:

Phase 4: Developing political solutions (this addresses question 1)
Phase 5: Selecting and implementing political solutions (this addresses questions 2 and 3)

The final three phases of the political engagement process address the following questions:

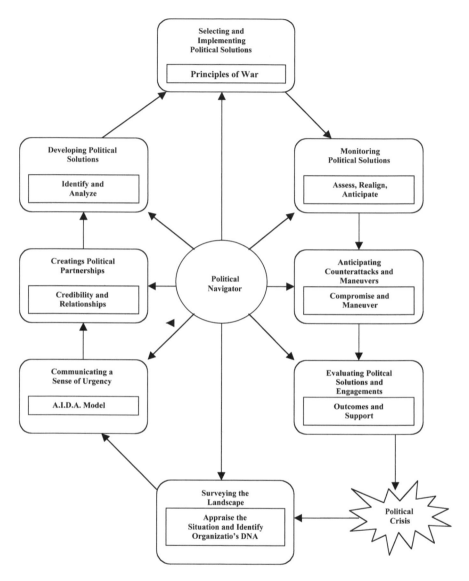

Figure 6.1. Eight Phases of the Political Engagement Process

1. How will you monitor the political solution?
2. What are your contingency plans if your political adversaries execute a counterattack or offensive maneuver?
3. Was the political solution successful in resolving the political conflict?

4. How will you determine the success of the political solution and whether your political objectives have been achieved?

Therefore, the final three phases of the political engagement process are:

Phase 6:   Monitoring political solutions (this addresses question 1)
Phase 7:   Anticipating counterattacks and maneuvers (this addresses question 2)
Phase 8:   Evaluating political solutions and political engagements (this addresses questions 3 and 4)

Phase 1: Surveying the Landscape

Question: What am I up against?

During this phase of a political engagement, you gather information that will help you figure out what has happened, how serious the situation is, and what should be done next. Additionally, it is helpful to identify strategies and actions that are appropriate during the remaining phases of the political engagement process (and see chapter 5).

There are several questions that can guide you in creating an initial response to the political crisis. They are as follows:

1. What just happened?
2. Why did it happen?
3. Who's involved and what are their motives?
4. Who will help me understand the situation better?
5. Who do I need to go to for information?
6. What is the definition of the political crisis?
7. What additional information do I need to gather that will help me in identifying a response?
8. What are my sources of power?
9. What are my next steps?

The next few questions will help you develop your short-term strategy for addressing the situation:

1. What is the political nature of the department, division, or unit where the political crisis occurred?
2. What are the connections, coalitions, and linkages in the affected department, division, or unit and how do they affect the situation?
3. What are my political objectives?
4. Whose support do I need to accomplish my political objectives?
5. Whose cooperation do I need to accomplish my political objectives?

6. What are the barriers to my political objectives?
7. What partnerships should be developed to ensure the success of my political objectives?
8. What are the goals, risks, assumptions, perceptions, and feelings of my partners about the political solution?
9. What is my influence strategy?

The answers to these questions will provide you with a practical way of gaining control of the situation and will help you develop a politically savvy approach for identifying initial steps in addressing the political crisis.

Question: What is the organization's DNA?

By addressing this question, you will be able to understand, discover, or analyze how things really work in the organization below the surface, behind the curtain, and inside the inner circle. During this phase, identify coalitions, connections, and linkages that will help you resolve the political conflict. Second, assess the strengths and weaknesses of the organization and its leadership and identify opportunities and threats facing the organization so that you can rely on this information to generate possible solutions to the political impasse. Next, conduct a relationship analysis to determine the intensity of relationship support for those individuals involved in the political conflict. Finally, rely on the information discussed in chapter 1 on understanding your organization and the needs and expectation of your clients to help you further analyze the organization and its leadership. Make certain that you take into account power relationships, tactics, and political behavior and that you employ influence tactics and political conflict principles, as well as utilize and understanding of conflict management styles, to execute this phase properly (see chapter 2).

Identifying Coalitions, Connections, and Linkages. Isolate those individuals who have developed alliances with powerful people in the organization. This helps you select individuals who can introduce you to important decisions makers and opinion leaders. Accordingly, identify those who are in the loop and those who are not. This will help you determine the individuals who can have the greatest influence in helping resolve the current crisis.

Identifying coalitions, connections, and linkages is extremely helpful because it tells you which individuals and groups work collectively together to achieve results. Simultaneously, it tells you which individuals and groups are no longer considered critical to the situation. Further, identifying coalitions, connections, and linkages can provide you insight into the organization's culture and work environments, which may prove critical as you identify and implement solutions that resolve the political impasse.

Analyzing the Strengths and Weaknesses of the Organization and Its Leadership. During this phase of the political engagement process, you need to conduct an analysis of the organization's internal and external environments, as discussed in chapter 4. This will provide information that clarifies the question "what is the organization's DNA?" Another purpose of this analysis is to identify the contingencies that will help you execute the political engagement and those that will hinder it. Furthermore, the analysis provides you information that will be critical in persuading others to support you during your political crisis.

The information gathered during your analysis will help you as you consider possible solutions to the political conflict. Further, this information will help you throughout the political engagement process because you will be better prepared to engage individuals that oppose you and wish to inflict their political will on you. Without a complete understanding of the organization, you are at a disadvantage in knowing how to proceed. Accordingly, you need information to identify partnerships and coalitions that will assist you later in the political engagement process. This information will help you develop a strategy and execution plan useful in achieving your desired results and outcomes. It will also help you remain focused as your political execution plan unfolds and will provide you information to assess and determine whether the political objectives have been achieved.

Phase 2: Communicating a Sense of Urgency

Question: How do I raise visibility and create a sense of urgency?

The second phase of the political engagement process is to successfully communicate a sense of urgency regarding the political conflict. Convince your colleagues, partners, and critical organizational leaders that the sky is falling and the political impasse is critical, and that a solution is needed now. Further, others must realize that, absent of immediate action in support of a political solution, your credibility and influence in the organization will be severely damaged and they will also be damaged and negatively affected. Collectively, everyone will be less effective in helping the organization achieve its strategic goals and objectives.

Without communicating a sense of urgency, the momentum for a political solution never materializes. This is because far too many organizational members are content with their current situation as long as the political crisis does not affect them. As a result, they are complacent. Under this condition, a political resolution is never obtained because few if any organizational members are willing to become actively involved. Consequently, it is difficult to cultivate support for political solution.

Implementing the A.I.D.A. Communications Model. To obtain the support you need, develop a communication strategy that produces the desired results. An important part of this activity is to identify your clients' responsiveness to the messages they receive. Four categories of response can be identified: attention, interests, desire, and action, and together these responses form the A.I.D.A. model. People's responses to such communications stimuli are a variable combination of knowledge (cognitive), attitudes and feelings (affective), and reactions (conative). Accordingly, communication messages that gain people's *attention* satisfy their cognitive (knowledge) curiosity. The message should also encourage *interest* and create *desire* to satisfy people's affective (attitudes and feelings) curiosity. Finally, messages that encourage *action* satisfy people's conative (behavior) curiosity.

Communication activities must first be designed to gain other people's attention. Once they are aware of the political crisis, communication activities must arouse their interest. This can be best accomplished by communicating the advantages, benefits, and values of resolving the political conflict and specifically how each participant personally benefits. Communication activities must reveal how a particular political solution can be beneficial to them and help them avoid future difficulties or resolve future conflicts. If successful, the communication strategy should produce a desire to participate in the conflict resolution process. People will then take action based upon their desire to resolve the political impasse.

Develop communication strategies that gain attention, arouse interest, and promote action. In this way, communication activities can be a call to action and help you solicit support that is critical to resolving the political conflict. Further, communication strategies maintain a common set of purposes: to inform and persuade of the advantages and benefits of a political solution.

To inform: The failure of many people involved in a political engagement is relying on inadequate or insufficient means for disseminating information. A successful communication strategy greatly enhances the probability of the adoption of political solution. Therefore, you should inform individuals of the advantages and benefits of a political solution very early in the political engagement process.

To persuade: Another purpose of a communication strategy is to persuade clients to take action such as participating in the design and development of a political solution. It may be as simple as recommending a particular solution that will help improve the situation. Whatever the communication activity is, it must be persuasive, appealing to one or more of the client's needs and expectations.

Creating a Guiding Coalition. A guiding coalition should be established to help you implement a political solution that resolves the conflict. This group will provide the leadership for resolving the conflict as well as provide the integrity, authority, and influence needed to successfully execute the political engagement. The first step in putting together a guiding coalition is to find the right membership. Four of the key characteristics needed of the guiding coalition key members are position power, expertise, credibility, and leadership. Having these four characteristics present in each member of the guiding coalition enables you to positively address the political impasse. This group should have enough key organizational leaders on board so that your political adversaries cannot easily block the political solutions that you advocate in the future. Additionally, this group should also have enough individuals with excellent reputations so that other organizational leaders will take group's pronouncements seriously. Such a group also provides you the visibility, strength, and credibility necessary to negotiate with your political adversaries.

Phase 3: Creating Political Partnerships

Question: What partnerships must be established to guarantee success?

During this phase of the political engagement process, you identified allies who will help you execute, monitor, adjust, and evaluate your political plan. This phase is known as the partnering phase and includes two primary components: the credibility phase and the relationship phase.

Credibility Phase. Political navigators are capable of establishing credibility within organizations in one of four ways. First, credibility can be transferred, most commonly by third-party referrals, which is often referred to as a network. Networks are a collection of individuals who can introduce you to key organizational leaders and decision makers. Typically, networks are informal in nature but they can also be structured activities. Second, political navigators can establish credibility by demonstrating the ability to solve complex problems resulting in the satisfying of people's needs and expectations. Third, credibility can be enhanced by demonstrating professional expertise that is valued by the organization. Doing so enables you to establish respect for your insight and particular area of expertise. Fourth, credibility can be developed via reputation, commonly by delivering results. Quite simply, credibility can be earned.

Demonstrating professional and organizational competence and expertise are essential to building credibility and a reputation with key decision makers. Political navigators demonstrate business acumen and address clients' attitudes, which establishes a level of credibility that becomes a source of power from which to make recommendations, provide suggestions, and share ideas useful in overcoming your current political impasse.

First, you are responsible for establishing credibility with decision makers, informal organizational leaders, and clients. The purpose of this subphase is to establish gravitas, which enables you to solicit assistance and advice. Additionally, this phase is used to demonstrate your "back wheel" expertise so that other people in the organization see you as a viable and serious political player. This will help others support you during the later phases of the political engagement process. Credibility can be developed by demonstrating your organizational awareness, demonstrating your conflict management skills, and demonstrating value-added service.

Demonstrating Organizational Awareness. To develop political acumen, you need to also understand the way organizations operate. Such insight will help you in identifying organizational needs, selecting solutions, implementing them, and evaluating them to make certain that you have achieved your political objectives. Political navigators know where to go for information, insight, recommendations, and coaching in order to avoid the pitfalls common in organizational life. Other benefits of organizational awareness include a better understanding of the political structure and decision-making procedures of the organization, both of which are essential in gaining the support needed to implement meaningful management action during a political conflict.

During political engagement, it is essential that you demonstrate your organizational awareness. resulting doing so, you will be communicating that you fully understand your organization, how to function within it, and that you are a person to be taken seriously. Demonstrating such awareness also reveals that you know whom go to for information, advice, and support. Again, this makes clear that you have connections in the organization and are not afraid to use them.

Demonstrating Conflict Management Skills. In chapter 2, we identified five conflict management styles to use when engaging in difficult political interactions and/or engagements. Each of the styles has its strengths and weaknesses and appropriate applications. However, those individuals interested in achieving desired results and outcomes while maintaining a responsive approach to the needs and expectations of others will function as political navigators. It is also important to emphasize conflict management skills as a political strategy and demonstrate them during any political engagement. In this way, you are encouraged to adopt an appropriate conflict management style as well as initiate conflict management activities as a political strategy.

Demonstrating a Value-added Service Philosophy. Establishing a value-added service philosophy requires you to be willing to place the needs and expectations of your clients above your own. Such a philosophy requires you to provide suggestions and recommendations that will resolve the current political impasse while enhancing the performance capacity of the organization and improving its overall effectiveness. A value-added service philosophy encourages you to address the current political situation in a collaborative and cooperative manner. Accordingly, the objectives of any political engagements should be to enhance performance capacity, improve organizational effectiveness, and resolve performance problems and organizational issues.

One of the best ways of establishing a value-added service philosophy is for you to participate in a personal reflection activity that allows you to be honest regarding your attitudes, beliefs, and feelings toward clients. You should write down why you are currently involved in this political engagement. Once you have identified motives, you should try to isolate a central theme (e.g., to improve organizational performance, improve the image of your department, protect resources, provide development opportunities for employees, improve the efficiency of your operation, develop a more competitive organization, or ensure organizational profitability). With a central theme identified, you are able to create a value-added service environment that is designed to accomplish your political objective(s).

Relationship Phase. During a political engagement, you are responsible for developing relationships with key decision makers, influencers, opinion leaders, and linkers if such relationships have yet to be cultivated. During a political engagement, it is critical that the relationships that you develop are not superficial but are based on a deep concern for the well-being of clients and are established through your sincere interest in and acceptance of your clients (see chapters 3 and 4). Such relationships help you develop a positive working environment that enhances communication. Therefore, you must be skilled in establishing positive environments and use communication skills that help you overcoming client resistance to new ideas and recommendations.

Becoming a political navigator requires you to create client exchanges that encourage open expressions of ideas and feelings, thereby creating an environment that fosters trust and feelings of security. As a result, clients realize that the lines of communication are open, increasing their willingness to discuss their problems with you. Finally, it is important to create a sharing environment that reduces the chances of skepticism and cynicism because it is built on trust and honesty.

The relationship phase requires you to develop a participatory communications climate, use your communications skills to solicit support, and establish rapport and trust with each client involved in the political engagement.

Participatory Communications Climate. Developing a participatory communications climate requires a shift in managerial style, resulting in relinquished control over clients, which allows them to participate as equal partners. Recognize that clients bring a great deal of experience to the organization and are a valuable resource to be acknowledged and tapped.

A participatory communications climate can only be developed when you encourage a free exchange of ideas, opinions, and feelings. Clients benefit from this type of environment because they feel more secure and can speak freely about issues affecting them. Such an environment is considered nonthreatening, comfortable, conducive to sharing, and even nurturing for client growth. A sharing environment goes beyond the superficial, demonstrates a deep concern for the well-being of clients, and is dedicated to the improvement of interpersonal relations.

Using Interpersonal Communications Skills. Once a positive communications climate has been established, several interpersonal communication skills are available that enhance client relationships. These skills help you gather client information, communicate points of view, share feelings, understand your clients, and provide a moment of silence so that clients can gather their thoughts. These skills serve as a guide in the client relationship process (see chapter 4).

Establish Rapport and Trust. Interpersonal relationships are difficult to develop and maintain. They can take a great toll on us personally and produce significant amounts of stress. However, they are absolutely critical to your success during a political engagement process. Chapter 3 discussed several strategies and ideas for establishing positive relationships that foster rapport and trust. These strategies and ideas should be interjected at this point in the political engagement process.

Phase 4: Developing Political Solutions

Question: What are the possible political solutions for resolving the political conflict?

Any political solution involves the exchange of value between parties for solutions of equal or greater value. A political solution is offered in exchange for time, energy, and personal commitment of other people. Acceptable and favorable exchange occurs when the political solution being offered is equal in value to the time, energy, and commitment returned by clients. If clients fail to perceive value that equals their time, energy, and commitment, they will not engage in the exchange. In other words, you can create value-added opportunities by developing exchanges that clients believe exceed what they are giving up. In order for this to occur, you must be skilled in planning and managing value-added exchanges with your clients.

During this phase, identify the values and benefits that clients receive from a political solution. Value statements should be developed that describe client rewards as a result of implementing the political solution. Value statements may be as simple as a sentence or two that describe the values and benefits clients glean from the transaction. This exercise helps clearly identify the positive values and benefits of the political solution and helps determine which solution offers the greatest merit within the organization.

There are three steps that should be followed when identifying a political solution: identifying possible solution, analyzing possible solutions, and selecting a solution, the latter of which is completed in Phase 5.

Identifying Possible Solutions. Generate as many ideas as possible to identify a solution. This activity should be conducted without evaluating or examining the ideas. The goal is to come up with as many solutions as possible.

Analyzing Possible Solutions. Once all the possible solutions have been identified, analyze each one using a set of criteria that serves as a standard or benchmark by which to filter each idea. Ideas that meet most of the criteria are grouped together for further analysis. The ideas that do not meet the status criteria should be filed for future consideration.

Phase 5: Selecting and Implementing Political Solutions

Question: What is the best solution for resolving the political conflict?

During this phase, test the solutions and that meet the benchmark criteria to decide their practicality and ease of application. Identify the cost and potential results of each a solution. This process will help you decide which of the possible solutions is best.

Another critical part of this phase is to name possible obstacles or barriers that may prevent applying a solution. As these barriers are named, look at them to decide the possible effects they may have on the various solutions. Identify actions to overcome obstacles or barriers, examining financial, human, and emotional costs. This process will help you decide whether the solution is appropriate. The outcome of this phase is that you identify the best alternative. Now you have an approach to follow in your quest to improve the political situation.

Question: What are the foundational principles for implementing political solutions?

Your principal responsibility during this phase of the political engagement process is to implement the best solution to the political conflict. During this phase, the focus is on testing the solution to determine its results. When doing this, choose the solution that has the opportunity for the highest degree of success. This strategy allows you to integrate the solution under the best possible conditions before applying it entirely.

Implementing solutions should be a slow and deliberate process to give you time to figure out the real outcomes. It is often a good idea to implement a solution in parts before introducing it entirely. Then you can refine and redesign the solution as needed.

Nine Principles of War. When you implement a solution, you incorporate foundational principles necessary for success. These principles are the *Nine Principles of War* and have been successfully used to guide military strategy and planning for over several centuries. These fundamental operational concepts are taught to young cadets at West Point and are consistently used to plan the application of U.S. combat power in foreign theaters of war. They serve as strategy guides for American military leaders as they think through military problems of deployment, strategy, and tactics. The same principles can serve as a strategy guide for you when you employ political engagements.

The nine principles of war applied to an organizational setting are:

1. Objective—direct every effort toward a clearly defined, decisive, an attainable goal.
2. Maneuver—place the competition at a disadvantage utilizing speed, efficiency, and strategy.
3. Simplicity—prepare clear, concise, and understandable efforts and missions to ensure thorough understanding.
4. Surprise—catch the competition off guard and in a manner for which they are unprepared.
5. Mass—concentrate the organization's resources to support success (and not mitigate failures).
6. Offense—seize, retain, and exploit the unit is initiative (act, do not react).
7. Unity of command—insure every effort or project has a clearly defined chain of authority and accountability.
8. Security—never permit your competition to acquire an unexpected advantage.
9. Economy of force—allocate minimal resources to nonessential efforts

As you implement a political solution, you should have a clearly defined, decisive, and obtainable result (objective). Implement the solution without warning (surprise) and make certain that everyone thoroughly and completely understands your actions (simplicity). Further, place your competition at a disadvantage (maneuver) and make certain that you are prepared for counterattacks and possible flanking maneuvers from your competition. Next, make certain that you have adequate resources and materials for a protracted engagement (mass). Prior to the implementation of the political solution, make certain that your partners and other organizational leaders are in full support of your actions (unity of command). Concentrate all of your effort at implementing the solution and make certain that you maintain your political will to succeed (offense). At all times, focus your full concentration on the objective and make certain that you are not focusing on unimportant, minor, and trivial issues (economy of force). Finally, never allow your competition to acquire an unexpected advantage during the implementation of the political solution (security).

Phase 6: Monitoring Political Solutions

Question: How will you monitor the political solution?

After a political solution has been implemented, it is critical that you monitor its success. This is achieved by gathering the opinions of a variety of individuals affected by the political conflict and its potential resolution. This is sometimes referred to as sampling. Once a sample has been gathered, determine the degree of satisfaction that people have with the political solution and determine if modifications and adjustments need to be made. If you determine that modifications are necessary, carry them out to realign and reestablish support for the political objective.

During the monitoring phase, is important to communicate and promote short-term wins that occurred as a result of implementing a political solution. Short-term wins refer to benefits that have been realized as a result of supporting the political solution. These are much like a small snowball that gathers momentum going down a hill and becomes a giant avalanche. They lay the foundation for wholesale acceptance of a political solution and help assure its success. Short-term wins provide evidence that sacrifices are worth the effort and reward political allies by providing positive public recognition. They solidify the support of the guiding coalition by providing concrete data on the viability of the solution and undermine cynics and self-serving individuals by demonstrating the benefits of the political solution. Short-term wins keep organizational leaders involved and supportive by providing evidence that the solution is on track. Finally, they build momentum, thus turning neutrals into supporters, reluctant supporters, into active helpers, and so forth.

During this phase, you must remain focused on the political objective. This is essential because a political solution can still fail if you take for granted its success and fail to maintain your concentration. Furthermore, you should be fully committed to implementing the political solution; otherwise your partners and other organizational leaders may withdraw their support, which would undercut and compromise the outcomes designed by the political solution. Finally, you need to maintain your political will and remain dogmatic and determined to integrate the political solution into the fabric of the organization.

Phase 7: Anticipating Counterattacks and Maneuvers

Question: What are your contingency plans if your political adversaries execute a counterattack or offensive maneuver?

You should never underestimate your political opponent and should always anticipate a counterattack and a flanking maneuver during this phase. One of the best ways to achieve these goals is to have a clearly defined contingency plan prepared so that you can employ a defensive action. At the first sign of a counterattack or offensive maneuver, you must immediately implement your contingency plan.

Always plan for the best, but prepare for the worst. This is a good motto to follow during this phase. And it is also important that you allow your political foe an opportunity to offer a compromise or an alternative plan to reduce the political conflict. This allows your opponent to save face during a potentially embarrassing situation. It's also important because you do not want to shame an opponent and create an enemy for life. This strategy also allows for an opportunity for a graceful exit from a politically damning situation. If, however, your political opponent is unwilling to offer an acceptable compromise, be willing to fully and completely execute your political solution. Do not be naïvely persuaded that a defeated opponent is not a dangerous opponent. If you are forced to continue with the political solution, completely and utterly destroy the will of your political opponent so that he or she will never again challenge you in the political arena. This may appear harsh and cruel, but it is a reality that you must embrace that will protect you from future political attacks.

Phase 8: Evaluating Political Solutions and Engagements

Question: How will you determine the success of the political solution and whether your political objectives have been achieved?

Once you have applied a solution, gather and compare the results. If the solution helps close the gap between the current and desired state, it can be considered a success. If, however, the gap remains the same, you need to consider alternative solutions. Regardless of the success or failure of a solution, the information and knowledge gained from carrying it out is invaluable. This value should be communicated to others in the organization to help them improve their understanding of the positive and negative impacts of the political engagement.

Any political engagement includes a means for measuring success, which is how others hold you accountable for your actions. In this way, you are constantly receiving feedback from others regarding suitability of the political solution. Feedback is not merely a superficial evaluation but is designed to identify the utility and shortcomings of a political solution. It can be solicited in a variety of ways. First, you can meet face-to-face with others to determine how effectively they believe their needs are being met. These people should be asked open-ended questions that allow them to reflect upon the values delivered by the political solution. Second, a representative sampling of individuals affected by the political solution can be identified, assembled in a focus group of no more than eight, and charged with the responsibility of determining whether or not the political solution is achieving its desired objectives. Such an analysis may produce a number of suggestions for improvement. As a result, you can develop strategies to modify the current solution or future solution. Possible changes might include: (1) modify a political solution to better meet people's needs and expectations; (2) modify their perceptions of the political solution.

After a decision has been made, individuals affected by the political solution may have second thoughts leading to a condition known as post-decision dissonance, a tension caused by uncertainty about the rightness of a choice. They may wonder if another alternative would have been the better choice. This doubt may seriously undermine their selection.

Post-decision dissonance is more likely when: (1) political solutions that were not selected have highly desirable attributes, (2) several desirable solutions were not chosen, or (3) the selection is irrevocable.

Most people experience some level of satisfaction or dissatisfaction with their selections. The level of satisfaction is directly related to the people's expectations of the solution chosen. If the political solution's outcomes match expectations, affected individuals will be satisfied. If, however, their selection fails to meet expectations, they will be dissatisfied.

You can help improve expectations by making certain that people's expectations are realistic and attainable. In fact, expectations should be stated conservatively so as not to generate false hopes. As always, follow-up and feedback are important. You should develop effective post-communication in order to reinforce client decisions. An abandoned client is a lost client. Finally, people's attitudes should be monitored to obtain an accurate picture of their perceptions of a political solution. To improve satisfaction, negative feedback should be incorporated when redesigning future political solutions.

Document the outcome of every solution tried and keep an active record of the dates and location of each one. This information will be an invalid resource in future political engagement efforts. Next, assess your current political support and evaluate your political strengths and weaknesses now that the political engagement has been completed. This is done in order to make certain that you have not damaged your credibility and influence as a result of the political engagement. This is a perfect time to determine whether or not you have enhanced your credibility and influence accordingly.

CONCLUSION

Politics often possess negative images in most of our minds; however, it is an important ingredient to the success of a manager. It is therefore essential that you develop a complete understanding of the eight phases of the political engagement process and how to execute them efficiently and effectively.

SEVEN

Development Plans and Self-Assessments for Political Navigators

This chapter begins with a comprehensive overview of the development planning process. This is useful in creating a self-directed learning contract, which is used for self-development. Four comprehensive self-assessment instruments are provided here to help you determine: gaps in your understanding of power, politics, and influence (Self-Assessments 1 and 2, covering material in chapters 1 and 2); your strengths and weaknesses in each of the five roles and responsibilities of a political navigator (Self-Assessment 3, chapter 3); your strengths and weaknesses in the seven skill areas of a political navigator (Self-Assessment 3, chapter 4); and your ability to apply political strategies (Self-Assessment 4, chapter 5).

CREATING DEVELOPMENT PLANS

The first step in creating development plans is to identify the competencies that need improving. This task includes comparing your current political competencies with desired competencies (see Self-Assessments 1–4). Competency areas that fall below minimum should become part of your development plan. However, it is also desirable for you to continue to develop competency areas in which you maintain a high level of proficiency. Therefore, development plans should be created that allow you to continue to develop your strengths. A development plan can help you acquire and transfer learning that helps you either overcome performance gaps or build on your strengths.

After you have completed the self-assessment instrument provided later in this chapter, you will have identified the skills/competencies to be changed in your development plan. Such a plan consists of seven steps (Figure 7.1):

- identifying learning objectives
- identifying learning resources and strategies
- developing learning activities
- identifying a target date for completion and implementing the development plan
- creating an on-the-job application strategy
- developing indicators of improvement and accomplishment
- providing rewards and recognition for accomplishment

This plan can be used along with formal scheduled training activities or as an independent and self-directed learning exercise.

Identifying Learning Objectives

Regardless of its type and length, every development plan has a set of desired outcomes. These outcomes are statements of what you should be able to know or do at the completion of the development plan. These outcomes are known as learning objectives and serve four primary functions: (1) they define the desired outcomes of the plan, (2) they serve as a guide to the selection of learning resources and strategies, (3) they serve as criteria for the development and selection of learning activities, and (4) they provide criteria for evaluating learning.

First, identify what you are going to learn. This activity is used to translate the identified skills and competencies into learning objectives. These objectives are written to describe what you will learn, not how you will learn them. Write a specific objective for each of the identified skills and competencies that needs improving. Depending on the type of learning objective, appropriate terminology should be used that is meaningful and descriptive (see Table 7.1). Learning objectives may be written to acquire skills, knowledge, attitudes, values, or understanding. The learning objectives identified will provide the focus of the development plan.

Learning objectives will guide and direct you in the learning process. Learning objectives also serve as the goals for your effort—a way to monitor your progress. Further, learning objectives should be used in selecting

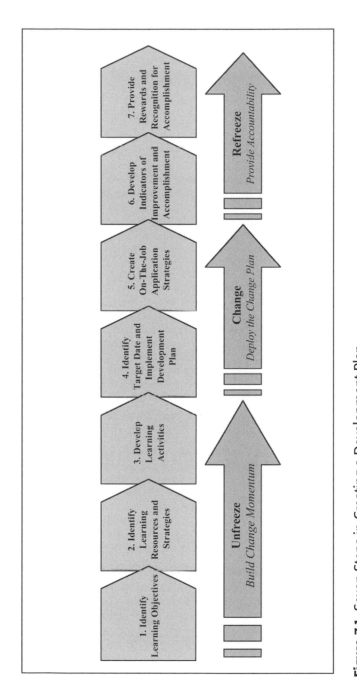

Figure 7.1. Seven Steps in Creating a Development Plan

Table 7.1 Learning Objectives by Cognitive, Affective, and Psychomotor Levels

Domain	Emphasis	Relevant Verbs
Cognitive	Knowledge	Count, recall, identify, recognize, point, acquire, recognize, repeat, quote, read, trace, quote, indicate, tabulate, identify, draw, define, distinguish, state, name, list, label, reproduce, order, record, recall
Cognitive	Comprehension	Associate, translate, compare, compute, contrast, describe, extrapolate, convert, interpret, estimate, interpret, classify, abstract, transform, select, indicate, illustrate, represent, formulate, explain, classify, comprehend
Cognitive	Application	Apply, calculate, illustrate, sequence, practice, utilize, complete, demonstrate, carry out, solve, prepare, operate, generalize, plan, repair, employ, explain, predict, demonstrate, instruct, compute, use, perform, implement, employ, solve
Cognitive	Analysis	Analyze, group, relate, transform, estimate, compare, observe, detect, classify, summarize, discover, discriminate, explore, infer, separate, distinguish, catalog, investigate, divide, breakdown, order, determine, differentiate, dissect, contrast, examine, interpret
Cognitive	Synthesis	Write, plan, integrate, design, create, develop, formulate, propose, specify, produce, prescribe, prepare, organize, theorize, design, build, systematize, produce, combine, summarize, restate, argue, propose, discuss, derive, relate, generalize, conclude, produce
Cognitive	Evaluation	Evaluate, critique, verify, grade, rank, recommend, assess, test, judge, rank, measure, specify, appraise, select, check, judge, justify, estimate, rate, select, test, determine, support, defend, criticize, weigh, assess
Affective		Agree, contribute, avoid, support, sustain, maintain, encourage, participate, cooperate, applaud, praise, help, assist, suggest, offer, join, unite
Psychomotor		Adjust, modify, repair, fix, taste, feel, smell, bend, twist, measure, calculate, perform, execute, operate, drive, control, maneuver, use, operate, move, shift

different learning resources (human or material) by which content and information are conveyed and the learning strategies are identified. They can also be used to select criteria for constructing tests and learning examinations used in evaluating your learning.

Because so many words and phrases we use are open to misinterpretation, writing learning objectives is a very difficult task. For example, learning objectives that describe your desire for further understanding, appreciation, and beliefs are virtually impossible to measure. Such objectives can best be communicated in words that are specific enough to preclude individual interpretation and at the level of learning desired. These are called action words (see Table 7.1).

A well-written learning objective describes the behavior that must be observed as a way of verifying that the intended learning has taken place. Accordingly, an objective should contain three components. They are:

- the desired learning
- the conditions or circumstances under which the task must be performed, or the learning duplicated
- the minimal acceptable level of learning or knowledge must be stated, which is often referred to as the standard of learning or knowledge (e.g., speed, accuracy, specifications of learning, or the consequences resulting from inadequate learning or knowledge)

Learning objectives can be written more clearly and precisely once the learning conditions, and standards have been identified.

A well-written learning objective should be clear and understandable, identify what you will learn, identify the acceptable level of performance for the learned behavior, describe the condition under which the performance will be measured, describe the observable behavior that will demonstrate that learning occurred, and be stated in such a way that the degree to which it is accomplished can be estimated or measured.

The following questions can help you develop well-written learning objectives:

1. What competency areas need improving or which strengths need further development?
2. What would you like to do differently in order to improve your effectiveness as a political navigator?
3. What do you need to learn or be able to do differently in order to achieve your development goals?
4. At what level would you like to demonstrate your learning (i.e., knowledge, comprehension, application, analysis, synthesis, or evaluation)?

5. Under what conditions will you demonstrate what you have learned (i.e., during a political interaction, political engagement, conflict resolution activity, or negotiation activity)?
6. Is the learning objective specific and clear?
7. When you achieve your learning objective can you measure what you have learned or observe a behavioral change? If not, rewrite the learning objective in order to make it measurable and observable.
8. What learning results or outcomes will occur when you achieve your learning objective?
9. Are the learning results or outcomes meaningful to you, others, and the organization? If yes, how so and in what form?

Identifying Learning Resources and Strategies

Next, describe how proposed learning objectives will be accomplished. This includes identifying learning resources and strategies. Both material and human resources should be considered for each of your learning objectives. Examples of common resources include books, handouts, newspapers, journal articles, lists of suggested readings, employees, superiors, mentors, resource persons, peers, professional trainers, videotapes, and cassettes. Strategies are the ways the identified resources will be used. This includes listening to lectures; participating in discussion groups; going to the library or learning resource center; keeping a journal of your political interactions; reading book chapters or articles on the identified competency area; making observations; and reflecting on political interactions and engagement activities to decide alternatives, options, actions, and strategies. Several resources and strategies may be listed for each learning objective.

When developing learning resources and strategies, the following questions serve as catalysts for quality improvement:

1. How will you accomplish your learning objective?
2. What resources (human or material) do you need to achieve your learning objective?
3. How will you obtain the necessary resources?
4. Are the resources proposed for each learning objective the most authoritative, reliable, and feasible available?
5. What learning support and reinforcement will you need to achieve your objective?
6. Whom can you rely on to help you achieve your objective?
7. Are there other resources—especially human—that should be considered?

When you select a resource, it should be the most suitable for the type of learning objective you are trying to accomplish. Each resource has its advantages and disadvantages and should be matched accordingly.

Developing Learning Activities

In formulating your development plan, it is essential that various learning activities be developed that provide you an opportunity to acquire the knowledge, skills, and behavior desired. These activities must be based on the identified learning objectives previously discussed as well as on the information collected and analyzed during self-assessment activities.

Learning activities may include games, debates, readings, presentations, group projects, panel discussions, reports and papers, and on-the-job application. Each should be selected based on the unique advantage they provide you. In short, learning objectives answer the question "where am I going?," while learning activities answer the question "how will I get there?"

Identifying a Target Date for Completion

Next, identify the date by which each learning objective will be completed. Establishing a date provides you with planning parameters and forces you to use time more efficiently.

The following questions will help you determine the target date for completing each learning objective:

- How much time will it take to complete each learning objective?
- What factors may influence completion (other projects, reports, vacations, and so forth)?
- When do you think you will complete your development plan?
- How important is it to acquire the competencies of a political navigator?

Implementing the Development Plan

Once a development plan has been developed, it must be implemented. Implementation includes sequencing the learning resources that will be used during completion of the development plan; participating in the learning activities; participating in formal learning or training activities, workshops, or seminars; and participating in on-the-job learning activities.

The following questions will help you implement your development plan:

- When will you begin your learning plan?
- How will you track your progress?
- What help or support will you need to implement it?
- How will you apply what you have learned on the job?
- When will you know that you need help in achieving your learning objectives?

- How will you integrate your learning plan into your daily work routine?
- When will you know that you have achieved your learning objectives?

Creating an On-the-Job Application Strategy

Identifying on-the-job applications is the next major phase of a development plan. It is during this phase that you identify exactly where and how you are going to apply new knowledge or skills. By completing this step you have identified the reason for engaging in a development plan in the first place. Unless this step is completed, learning will not be applied in a consistent manner.

Developing Indicators of Improvement or Accomplishment

Next, identify the indicators of the improvement or accomplishment that has occurred as a result of learning. This step helps you know when you have successfully achieved your learning objectives. Indicators can be expressed in terms of successful completion of tasks, observable behaviors, time measurement, and so on. Normally, indicators of improvement or accomplishment consist of one of six levels discussed earlier: knowledge, comprehension, application, analysis, synthesis, or evaluation.

To demonstrate the degree to which you have achieved each learning objective, identify the type of indicators you will use. The type of learning objective identified will determine the nature of evidence needed to provide the indicator. Indicators include improving skills, judging the quality of a performance, obtaining colleagues' observations of your performance during political interactions and engagements, applying a new skill during a political interaction or engagement, and so forth.

The following questions will help you identify indicators of accomplishment:

1. How will you know when you have successfully achieved your learning objectives?
2. Whom will you rely on to determine that you have successfully completed your learning objectives?
3. What evidence will you use to judge that you have successfully completed your learning objectives?
4. How will you measure what you have learned or are able to do differently?

5. How will you measure the results produced by your new knowledge, skills, or attitude?

The following are examples of indicators for different types of learning objectives:

Type of Objective	Examples of Indicators
Attitudes	Attitudinal rating scales, performance in real situations, role playing, simulation games, critical incident cases with feedback from participants and/or observers
Knowledge	Reports of knowledge acquired, as in journals, essays, examinations, oral presentations, audiovisual presentations
Skills	Results from performance exercises, videotaped role plays critiqued by observers, peer critiques of actual performance, employees' observations, superiors' observations, formal assessment activities
Understanding	Examples of utilization of knowledge in solving problems, projects, decision-making activities, and feedback and coaching opportunities
Values	Value rating scales, performance in value identification groups, critical incident cases, simulation exercises with feedback from participants and/or observers

Providing Rewards and Recognition for Accomplishment

Once a development plan has been successfully completed, you should celebrate. In this way, you receive an intrinsic reward for the successful acquisition of knowledge and skills. When learning is viewed as a developmental activity rather than a punitive action, this step is essential and it helps motivate you to apply new skills and competencies on the job. The following questions will help you celebrate your successes:

- How will you reward yourself for achieving your learning objectives?
- How will you celebrate your new learning, increased skills, and improved attitude?

Finally, competency improvement through learning should be formally recognized and rewarded by the organization. However, your true reward is improved credibility and influence in the organization, which should lead to increased job satisfaction and personal fulfillment.

POLITICAL NAVIGATOR SELF-ASSESSMENT

The development planning process begins by identifying the skills and competencies that need improving. To accomplish this you need to engage in a self-reflective process that helps you determine your strengths and weaknesses. In the next few pages, several self-reflective instruments will be identified.

Self-Assessment 1 is a self-audit designed to help you identify your primary motivation for developing political competency; your overall competency as political navigator; your understanding and application of power in your organization; the political climate of your organization; political tactics that you commonly use; and your personal communication style. Self-Assessment 2 allows you to conduct a self-assessment of your understanding of the power, politics, and influence on organizations. Self-Assessment 3 allows you to identify your strengths and weaknesses in each of the five roles and responsibilities of a political navigator discussed in chapter 3. This instrument also enables you to assess your strengths and weaknesses in the seven skills areas of a political navigator outlined in chapter 4. Self-Assessment 4 enables you to rank your proficiency in applying preparation, protection, effectiveness, and competency strategies identified in chapter 5. This self-assessment will help you determine how well you perform a variety of political strategies. Once you have completed these a four self-assessments, you can create a development plan that builds on your strengths and improves your weaknesses. The eight-step development planning process discussed previously is an ideal way of enhancing your proficiency as a political navigator.

SELF-ASSESSMENT 1: SELF-AUDIT (CHAPTERS 1 AND 2)

1. Which of the following is your primary motivation for developing political competence? Please check as many as apply.
   ☐ Advancing my career
   ☐ Self-defense
   ☐ Enhancing my self-esteem
   ☐ Building credibility in my organization
   ☐ Enhancing influence in my organization
   ☐ Improving political interaction
   ☐ Improving political engagement
   ☐ Improving desired results and outcomes
   ☐ Meeting the needs and expectation of others

2. Which of the following best describes your current competence as a political navigator?
   ☐ Conscious competent
   ☐ Unconscious incompetent
   ☐ Unconscious competent
   ☐ Conscious incompetent

3. Which of the following sources of power do you rely on to achieve desired results or outcomes? Please check as many as apply.
   ☐ Legitimate power
   ☐ Reward power
   ☐ Coercive power
   ☐ Expert power
   ☐ Referent power

4. Power is used in your organization for which of the following reasons? Please check as many as apply.
   ☐ Fear of uncertainty
   ☐ Erosion of position
   ☐ Perceived threat
   ☐ Ambiguous goals
   ☐ Scarce resources
   ☐ Technological and environmental uncertainties
   ☐ Nonprogrammed decisions
   ☐ Organizational change

5. The political climate in your organization would be best characterized as:
   ☐ Fairyland
   ☐ Team-oriented
   ☐ Competitive
   ☐ Pathological

6. Which of following political tactics do you use most to influence individuals within your organization?
   - ☐ Inspirational appeals
   - ☐ Consultation
   - ☐ Personal appeals
   - ☐ Exchange
   - ☐ Pressure
   - ☐ Integration
   - ☐ Rational persuasion
   - ☐ Coalitions
   - ☐ Pressure tactics
   - ☐ Legitimizing

7. Your interpersonal communication style most close resembles which of the following?
   - ☐ Driver
   - ☐ Expressive
   - ☐ Analytical
   - ☐ Amiable

SELF-ASSESSMENT 2: POLITICAL NAVIGATORS' UNDERSTANDINGS OF POWER, POLITICS, AND INFLUENCE IN ORGANIZATIONS (CHAPTER 2)

Read each of the following statements carefully, determine your response, and CIRCLE the appropriate number.	*Poor*	*Fair*	*Average*	*Good*	*Excellent*
1. Understanding of Your Organization	1	2	3	4	5
2. Understanding of the Political Interaction Process	1	2	3	4	5
3. Understanding of the Political Engagement Process	1	2	3	4	5
4. Understanding of Your Clients	1	2	3	4	5
5. Understanding of the Needs and Expectations of Your Clients	1	2	3	4	5
6. Understanding of Power	1	2	3	4	5
7. Understanding of Political Strategy	1	2	3	4	5

SELF-ASSESSMENT 3: POLITICAL NAVIGATORS' ROLES, RESPONSIBILITIES, AND SKILLS (CHAPTERS 3 AND 4)

Please rank the following and CIRCLE the appropriate number.	*Poor*	*Fair*	*Average*	*Good*	*Excellent*
Your Ability to Execute the Roles of Political Navigators					
1. Relationship Builder	1	2	3	4	5
2. Assertive Communicator	1	2	3	4	5
3. Negotiator	1	2	3	4	5
4. Organizational Expert	1	2	3	4	5
5. Partnership Builder	1	2	3	4	5
Your Ability to Execute the Responsibilities of Political Navigators					
1. Developing Synergistic Relationships	1	2	3	4	5
2. Improving Organizational Communication	1	2	3	4	5
3. Demonstrating Organizational Knowledge	1	2	3	4	5
4. Identifying and Solving Problems	1	2	3	4	5
5. Building Consensus and Commitment	1	2	3	4	5
Your Ability to Perform the Skills of Political Navigators					
1. Relationship Skills	1	2	3	4	5
2. Communications Skills	1	2	3	4	5
3. Conflict Resolution Skills	1	2	3	4	5
4. Partnership Skills	1	2	3	4	5
5. Observation Skills	1	2	3	4	5
6. Organizational Understanding Skills	1	2	3	4	5
7. Political Thinking Skills	1	2	3	4	5

SELF-ASSESSMENT 4: POLITICAL NAVIGATORS' RANKING OF POLITICAL STRATEGIES (CHAPTER 5)

Using the following rating scale, please rate your proficiency for the following strategies. Determine your response and CIRCLE the appropriate number.	Poor	Fair	Average	Good	Excellent
PREPARATION STRATEGIES					
1. Observing, Observing, Observing	1	2	3	4	5
2. Identifying the Power	1	2	3	4	5
3. Developing Integration Skills	1	2	3	4	5
4. Building Coalitions in the Organization	1	2	3	4	5
5. Developing Contacts	1	2	3	4	5
6. Keeping Your Powder Dry	1	2	3	4	5
7. Building Rapport with the "Right People"	1	2	3	4	5
8. Embracing Your Worst Political Adversary as a Human Being	1	2	3	4	5
9. Developing Finesse	1	2	3	4	5
10. Developing Favor Banks	1	2	3	4	5
11. Knowing the Strengths/Weaknesses of Your Conflict Management Style	1	2	3	4	5
PROTECTION STRATEGIES					
1. Being Nice and Friendly	1	2	3	4	5
2. Picking Your Battles	1	2	3	4	5
3. Utilizing the Crazy Person Strategy	1	2	3	4	5
4. Knowing When to Fold Them	1	2	3	4	5
5. Keeping Your Distance	1	2	3	4	5
6. Demonstrating Poise	1	2	3	4	5
7. Avoiding Public Confrontations	1	2	3	4	5

EFFECTIVENESS STRATEGIES

1. Doing the Unexpected	1	2	3	4	5
2. Advocating Solutions	1	2	3	4	5
3. Providing Objective Observations	1	2	3	4	5
4. Guarding against Complacency	1	2	3	4	5
5. Securing the High Ground	1	2	3	4	5
6. Developing Finesse	1	2	3	4	5
7. Thinking Like a Chess Player	1	2	3	4	5
8. Playing It Close to the Vest	1	2	3	4	5
9. Standing Your Ground	1	2	3	4	5
10. Impeccable Timing	1	2	3	4	5
11. Balancing Results and Relationships	1	2	3	4	5
12. Thinking on your Feet	1	2	3	4	5
13. Asking Well-Placed Reflective Questions	1	2	3	4	5
14. Letting It Go	1	2	3	4	5

COMPETENCY STRATEGIES

1. Creating a Thirty-Second Commercial	1	2	3	4	5
2. Identifying with Clients	1	2	3	4	5
3. Practicing Reciprocity	1	2	3	4	5
4. Developing Mutual Interests with Clients	1	2	3	4	5
5. Becoming a Scout	1	2	3	4	5
6. Becoming a Strategic Partner	1	2	3	4	5
7. Becoming an Influencer	1	2	3	4	5
8. Becoming a Strategist	1	2	3	4	5
9. Becoming a Problem Solver	1	2	3	4	5
10. Becoming a Communicator	1	2	3	4	5
11. Becoming a Collaborator	1	2	3	4	5
12. Improving Client Relationships through Learning	1	2	3	4	5

CONCLUSION

Becoming a conscious competent political navigator requires you to develop a strategy for continuous improvement. This can best be achieved by creating a development plan designed to enhance your knowledge, skills, and competencies as a political navigator. Identifying your strengths and weaknesses can be ascertained by completing the four assessment instruments provided. You should then create a development plan using the eight-step process previously discussed. At the conclusion of this activity, you will have created a long-term development strategy useful in becoming a conscious competent political navigator.

EIGHT

Resources for Political Navigators

This chapter identifies a number of important publications, organizations, Web sites, and journals. They are beneficial in your journey to becoming a political navigator because they provide information that will be critical to continuous development and learning. The resources are listed under the following topical headings: communications; conflict resolution; conflict styles; consensus building; development plans and learning principles; negotiations; organizational development and organizations; partnerships; political thinking; power, politics, and influence; problem solving; and relationship building.

BOOKS AND ARTICLES

Communications

Argenti, Paul. A., and Janis Forman. *The Power of Corporate Communications: Crafting a Voice and Image of Your Business.* New York: McGraw-Hill, 2002.

Bolton, Robert. *People Skills: How to Assert Yourself, Listen to Others, and Resolve Conflicts.* New York: Simon and Schuster, 1986.

Bolton, Robert, and Dorothy Grover Bolton. *People Styles at Work: Making Bad Relationships Good and Good Relationships Better.* New York: AMA-COM, 1996.

Dawson, Roger. *Secrets of Power Persuasion: Everything You Will Ever Need to Get the Things You Ever Want.* 2nd ed. Englewood Cliffs, NJ: Prentice Hall Press, 2001.

Leed, Dorothy. *The 7 Powers of Questions: Secrets to Successful Communications in Life and at Work.* New York: Perigee Books, 2000.

McKay, Matthew, Martha Davis, and Patrick Fanning. *Messages: The Communications Skills Book.* 2nd ed. Oakland, CA: New Harbinger Publications, 1995.

Nichols, Ralph G., Leonard A. Stevens, Fernando Bartolome, and Chris Argyris. *Harvard Business Review on Effective Communications.* Cambridge, MA: Harvard Business School Press, 1999.

Conflict Resolution

Block, Peter. *Flawless Consulting: A Guide to Getting Your Expertise Used.* 2nd ed. San Diego: Pfeiffer, 1999.

Cloke, Kenneth, and Joan Goldsmith. *Resolving Conflicts at Work: A Complete Guide for Everyone on the Job.* San Francisco: Jossey-Bass, 2001.

Dana, Daniel. *Conflict Resolution.* New York: McGraw-Hill, 2000.

Deutsch, Morton, and Peter. T. Coleman. *Handbook of Conflict Resolution: Theory and Practice.* San Francisco: Jossey-Bass, 2000.

Harvard Business Review on Negotiations and Conflict Resolution. Cambridge, MA: Harvard Business School Press, 2000.

Greenleaf, Robert K. *On Becoming a Servant Leader.* San Francisco: Jossey-Bass, 1996.

Maurer, Richard. *Beyond the Wall of Resistance: Unconventional Strategies That Build Support for Change.* Austin, TX: Bard Books, 1996.

Mayer, Bernard S. *The Dynamics of Conflict Resolution: A Practitioner's Guide.* San Francisco: Jossey-Bass, 2000.

Ury, Wilhorn L. *The Third Side: Why We Fight and How We Can Stop.* New York: Penguin Putnam, 2000.

Weeks, Dudley. *The Eight Essential Steps in Conflict Resolution: Preserving Relationships at Work, at Home, and in the Community.* Los Angeles: J. P. Tarcher, 1994.

Conflict Styles

Dixit, Avinash K., and Barry J. Nalebuff. *Thinking Strategically: A Comparative Edge in Business: Politics, and Everyday Life.* New York: W. W. Norton and Co., 1991.

Leas, Speed B. *Discover Your Conflict Management Style.* Herndon: Alban Institute, 1998.

Consensus Building

Harbison, John R., and Peter Pekar. *Smart Alliances: A Practical Guide to Repeatable Success.* San Francisco: Jossey-Bass, 1998.

Kaner, Sam, Lenny Lind, Catherine Toldi, Sarah Fisk, and Duane Berger. *A Facilitator's Guide to Participatory Decision-Making.* Gabriola Island, BC, Canada: New Society Publishers, 1996.

Kuglin, Fred A., and Jeff Hook. *Building, Leading, and Managing Strategic Alliances: How to Work Effectively and Profitably with Partner Companies.* New York: American Management Association, 2002.

Maslow, Abrhom H. "A Theory of Human Motivation." *Psychological Review* (July 1943) 370–96.

Straus, David, and Thomas C. Layton. *How to Make Collaboration Work: Powerful Ways to Build Consensus, Solve Problems, and Make Decisions.* San Francisco: Berrett-Koehler Publishers, 2001.

Susskind, Lawrence, Sarah McKearnan, and Jennifer Thomas-Larmer. *The Consensus Building Handbook: A Comprehensive Guide to Reaching Agreement.* Thousand Oaks, CA: Sage Publications, 1999.

Development Plans and Learning Principles

Argyris, Chris, and Donald Schon. *Organizational Learning II: A Theory of Action Perspective.* Reading, MA: Addison-Wesley, 1996.

Brinkerhoff, Robert O., and Anne M. Apking. *High Impact Learning: Strategies for Leveraging Business Results from Training.* Cambridge, MA: Perseus, 2001.

Brinkerhoff, Robert O., and Steven J. Gill. *The Learning Alliance.* San Francisco: Jossey-Bass, 1994.

Buckingham, Marcus, and Donald O. Clifton. *Now, Discover Your Strengths.* New York: Free Press, 2001.

Gilley, Jerry W., and Anu Maycunich. *Beyond the Learning Organization: Creating a Culture of Continuous Development through State-of-the-Art-Human Resource Practices.* Cambridge, MA: Perseus, 2000.

Knowles, Malcom S. *Self-Directed Learning.* New York: Association Press, 1975.

Mager, Robert F. *Preparing Instructional Objectives.* 2nd ed. Belmont, CA: Fearon, 1975.

Marquardt, Michael J. *Action Learning in Action: Transforming Problems and People for World-Class Organizational Learning.* Palo Alto, CA: Davies-Black Publishing, 1999.

Vaile, Peter. *Learning as a Way of Being.* San Francisco: Jossey-Bass, 1996.
Zemke, Ron, & Sue Zemke. "Adult Learning: What Do We Know for Sure?" *Training* 32, no. 6 (1995): 31–40.

Negotiations

Dawson, Roger. *Secrets of Power Negotiating.* 2nd ed. Princeton, NJ: Career Press, 2000.
Fisher, Roger, William L. Ury. *Getting to Yes: Negotiating Agreements without Giving in.* New York and New Rutherford, NJ: Penguin, 1991.
Harvard Business Essentials Guide to Negotiations. Cambridge, MA: Harvard Business School Press, 2003.
Harvard Business Review on Negotiations and Conflict Resolution. Cambridge, MA: Harvard Business School Press, 2000.
Lewicki, Roy J., Bruce Barry, David M. Saunders, and John W. Minton. *Essential Negotiation.* 3rd ed. New York: McGraw-Hill/Irwin, 2003.
Shell, G. Richard. *Bargaining for Advantage: Negotiation Strategy for Reasonable People.* New Rutherford, NJ: Penguin Books, 2000.
Stone, Douglas, Bruce Patton, Sheila Heen, and Roger Fisher. *Difficult Conversations: How to Discuss What Matters Most.* New Rutherford, NJ: Penguin Putnam, 2000.
Ury, William L. *Getting Past No: Negotiating Your Way from Confrontation to Cooperation.* New York: Bantam, 1993.

Organizational Development and Organizations

Anderson, Dean, and Linda A. Anderson. *Beyond Change Management: Advanced Strategies for Today's Transformational Leader.* San Francisco: Pfeiffer, 2001.
Bolman, Lee. G., and Terrance E. Deal. *Reframing Organizations: Artistry, Choice, and Leadership.* 3rd ed. San Francisco: Jossey-Bass, 2003.
Burke, W. Warren. *Organizational Development: A Process of Learning and Changing.* Reading, MA: Addison-Wesley, 1992.
Burke, W. Warren. *Organization Change: Theory and Practice.* Thousand Oaks, CA: Sage Publications, 2002.
Cummings, Thomas G., and Christopher G. Worley. *Organizational Development and Change.* 8th ed. Cincinnati: South-Western College Publishing, 2001.
French, Wendell L., and Cecil H. Bell, Jr. *Organizational Development: Behavioral Science Interventions for Organizational Improvement.* 6th ed., Englewood Cliffs, NJ: Prentice Hall, 1998.
French, Wendell L., and Cecil H. Bell, Jr. *Organizational Development: Behavioral Science Interventions for Organizational Improvement.* Englewood Cliffs, NJ: Prentice Hall, 1999.

Galbraith, Jay R., and Edward D. Lawler, III. *Organizing for the Future.* San Francisco, CA: Jossey-Bass, 1993.

Gibson, James L., John M. Ivancevich, James H. Donnelly, and Robert Konopaske. *Organizations: Behavior, Structure, Process.* 9th ed. New York: McGraw-Hill, 1999.

Ulrich, David. *Human Resource Champions.* Cambridge, MA: Harvard Business School Press, 1997.

Partnerships

Bellman, Geoffrey M. "Partnership Phase: Forming Partnerships." Pp. 39–53 in *Moving from Training to Performance: A Practical Guide,* eds. D. G. Robinson and J. C. Robinson. San Francisco: Berrett-Koehler Publishers, 1998.

Gerdes, Sarah. *Navigating the Partnership Maze: Creating Alliances That Work.* New York: McGraw-Hill, 2002.

Kuglin, Fred. A., and Jeff. Hook. *Building, Leading, and Managing Strategic Alliances: How to Work Effectively and Profitably with Partner Companies.* New York: American Management Association, 2002

LeBoeuf, Michael. *Getting Results: The Secret to Motivating Yourself and Others.* New York: Berkeley Books, 1985.

Rigsbee, Edward. *Developing Strategic Alliances.* Fredericton, New Brunswick, Canada: Crisp Publications, 2000.

Stokes, Leonard. *Accounting for Partnerships.* Cincinnati: South-Western College Publishing, 2002.

Tisch, Johnathan and Karl Weber. *The Power of We: Succeeding through Partnerships.* New York: Wiley, 2004.

Political Thinking

Tinder, Glenn. *Political Thinking: The Perennial Questions*6th ed. New York: Longman, 2003.

Power, Politics, and Influence

Bauer, Joel, and Mark Levy. *How to Persuade People Who Don't Want to Be Persuaded: Get What You Want—Every Time!* New York: Wiley, 2004.

Bellman, Geoffrey M. *Getting Things Done When You Are Not in Charge.* San Francisco: Berrett-Koehler Publishers, 2001.

Block, Peter. *The Empowered Manager: Positive Political Skills at Work.* San Francisco: Jossey-Bass, 1987.

Bolman, Lee. G., and Terrence E. Deal. *Reframing Organizations: Artistry, Choice, and Leadership.* 3rd ed. San Francisco: Jossey-Bass, 2003.

Cialdini, Robert B. *Influence: The Psychology of Persuasion.* New York: Perennial Currents, 1998.

Cohen, Allen R., and David L. Bradford. *Influence without Authority.* New York: Wiley, 1991.

Falbe, Cecilia M., and Gary A. Yukl. "Consequences for Managers of Using Single Influence Tactics and Combinations of Tactics." *Academy of Management Journal* no. 3 (1992): 647–661.

French, John R. P., and Bertram H. Raven. "The Bases of Social Power." In *Studies of Social Power*, ed. D. Cartwright. Ann Arbor, MI: Institute for Social Research, 1959.

Greene, Robert. *The 48 Laws of Power.* New Rutherford, NJ: Penguin Putnam, 2000.

———. *The Art of Seduction.* New Rutherford, NJ: Penguin Putnam, 2003.

Kotter, John P. *Power and Influence.* New York: Free Press, 1985.

Pfeffer, J. *Managing with Power: Politics and Influence in Organizations.* Cambridge, MA: Harvard Business School Press, 1994.

Reardon, Kathleen K. *The Secret Handshake: Mastering the Politics of the Business Inner Circle.* New York: Doubleday, 2001.

Soloman, Robert C., and Fernando Flores. *Building Trust: In Business, Politics, Relationships, and Life.* New York: Oxford University Press, 2003.

Vengel, Alan A. *The Influence Edge: How to Persuade Others to Help You Achieve Your Goals.* San Francisco: Berrett-Koehler Publishers, 2001.

Wilson, Graham K. *Business and politics: A Comparative Introduction.* 3rd ed. Chatham, NJ: Chatham House Publishers, 2003.

Yukl, Gary M., and Cecilia M. Falbe. "Influence Tactics and Objectives in Upward, Downward, and Lateral Influence Attempts." *Journal of Applied Psychology* 75, no. 3 (1990): 133–148.

Problem Solving

Jones, Morgan D. *The Thinker's Toolkit: 14 Powerful Techniques for Solving Problems.* New York: Three Rivers Press, 1998.

Larson, Loren C. *Problem Solving through Problems.* New York: Springer, 1983.

Rossett, Allison. *First Things Fast: A Handbook for Performance Analysis.* San Francisco: Pfeiffer, 1999.

Zeitz, Paul. *The Art and Craft of Problem-Solving.* New York: Wiley, 1999.

Relationship Building

Bolton, Robert. *People Skills: How to Assert Yourself, Listen to Others, and Resolve Conflicts.* New York: Simon and Schuster, 1986.

Bolton, Robert, and Dorothy Grover Bolton. *People Styles at Work: Making Bad Relationships Good and Good Relationships Better.* New York: AMA-COM, 1996.

Fisher, Roger, and Scott Brown. *Getting Together: Building Relationships as We Negotiate.* New Rutherford, NJ: Penguin, 1989.

Goleman, Daniel. *Working with Emotional Intelligence.* New York: Bantam Books, 1998.

Thoele, Sue P., and Cynthia L. Wall. *The Courage to Trust: A Guide to Building Deep and Lasting Relationships.* Oakland, CA: New Harbinger Publications, 2005.

ORGANIZATIONS, JOURNALS, AND WEB SITES

Communications

National Communication Association, 1765 N Street, NW, Washington, DC, 20036. Phone: 202-464-4622. Web site: www.natcom.org

Journals

- *Communication and Critical/Cultural Studies*
- *Communication Education*
- *Communication Monographs*
- *Journal of Applied Communication Research*
- *Review of Communication*

Conflict Resolution

Association for Conflict Resolution, 1015 18th Street, NW, Suite 1150, Washington, DC, 20036. Phone: 202-464-9700.Web site: www.ACRnet.org

Journals

- *ACResolution Magazine*
- *Conflict Resolution Quarterly*

Consensus Building

Consensus Building Institute, 238 Main Street, Suite 400, Cambridge, MA, 02142. Phone: 617-492-1414. Web site: www.cbuilding.org

Journals

- None identified

Development Plans and Learning Principles

American Society for Training and Development: Linking People, Learning and Performance, 1640 King Street, Box 1443, Alexandria, VA, 22313–2043. Phone: 703-683-8100. Web site: www.astd.org

Journals

- *Training and Development*
- *Training Magazine*

Academy of Human Resource Development, College of Technology, Bowling Green State University, Bowling Green, OH, 43403. Phone: 419-372-9155. Web site: www.ahrd.org

Journals

- *Advances in Developing Human Resources*
- *Human Resource Development International*
- *Human Resource Development Quarterly*
- *Human Resource Development Review*

International Society for Performance Improvement, 1400 Spring Street, Suite 260, Silver Spring, MD, 20910. Phone: 301-587-8570. Web site: www.ispi.org

Journals

- *Performance Improvement Journal*
- *Performance Improvement Quarterly*

Negotiations

Programs on Negotiations at Harvard Law School, 1563 Massachusetts Avenue, Cambridge, MA, 02138. Web site: www.pon.havard.edu/research

Journals

- *Harvard Negotiation Law Review*
- *Negotiation Journal*
- *Negotiation Newsletter*

Organizational Development and Organizations

Organization Development Network, 71 Valley Street, Suite 301, South Orange, NJ, 07079–2825. Phone: 973-763-7337. Web site: www.ODNetwork.org

Journals

- *Journal of Change Management*
- *Journal of Organizational Development*
- *Leadership and Organizational Development*
- *Organization Development Journal*

Index

About the Author

JERRY W. GILLEY is Professor and Chair of the Organizational Performance and Change and Human Resource Studies programs at Colorado State University. Previously on the faculty at Iowa State University, Western Michigan University, and the University of Nebraska-Lincoln, he also served as Principal and Director of Organization and Professional Development for Mercer Human Resource Consulting. Currently serving as President of the Academy of Human Resource Development, he is author, co-author, and co-editor of dozens of articles and over a dozen books, including *The Performance Challenge, Beyond the Learning Organization, Stop Managing, Start Coaching,* and *Organizational Learning, Preformance, and Change,* recipient of the Academy of Human Resource Development book-of-the-year award in 2000.